First World War
and Army of Occupation
War Diary
France, Belgium and Germany

49 DIVISION
Divisional Troops
49 Sanitary Section
7 April 1915 - 31 March 1917

WO95/2790/2

The Naval & Military Press Ltd
www.nmarchive.com
Published in association with The National Archives

Published by

The Naval & Military Press Ltd

Unit 10 Ridgewood Industrial Park,
Uckfield, East Sussex,
TN22 5QE England
Tel: +44 (0) 1825 749494

www.naval-military-press.com
www.nmarchive.com

This diary has been reprinted in facsimile from the original. Any imperfections are inevitably reproduced and the quality may fall short of modern type and cartographic standards.

© Crown Copyright
Images reproduced by permission of The National Archives, London, England, 2015.

Contents

Document type	Place/Title	Date From	Date To
Heading	WO95/2790/2 49 Sanitary Section.		
Heading	49th Division 49th W.R. Divl Sanitary Secn Apr 1915-Apr 1917 To 2 Army		
Heading	Sanitary 49th (W.R) Division Vol I		
War Diary	York.	07/04/1915	13/04/1915
War Diary	Havre	14/04/1915	05/05/1915
War Diary	Fleurbaix	06/05/1915	31/05/1915
Map	Sailly Sans La		
Miscellaneous	Date.		
Heading	49th Division West Riding Fld Amb Workshop Unit Lieut Vol I0-3.4.15		
Heading	War Diary Of West Riding Field Ambulance Workshop Unit A.S.C From April 10/16 To April 30/15		
Miscellaneous	West Riding F.A.W.U G.S Harris 1/20000 April 10th 1915	10/04/1915	10/04/1915
Heading	49th (W.R) Field Ambulance Workshop Vol II May 1915		
Miscellaneous	49th (W.R) Field Ambulance Workshop Vol II May 1915		
Heading	War Diary Of West Riding Field Ambulance Workshop Unit (A.S.C.) From May 1st To May 31st 1915		
Miscellaneous	Parked At Estaires.		
Heading	49th Division Cut Not Copied Vol II June 1915		
War Diary	Fleurbaix	01/06/1915	26/06/1915
War Diary	Doulieu	27/06/1915	28/06/1915
War Diary	Merris.	29/06/1915	29/06/1915
War Diary	Proven	30/06/1915	30/06/1915
Heading	49th Division Sanitary Sect. 49th Division Vol III		
War Diary	Proven	01/07/1915	07/07/1915
War Diary	Nr Poperinghe	08/07/1915	31/07/1915
Heading	49th Division 49th Divl: Sanitary Section Vol IV Aug & Sept 15		
War Diary	Nr Poperinghe	01/08/1915	30/09/1915
Heading	49th Division Summarised 49th Sanitary Section Vol V Oct 15		
War Diary	Nr Poperinghe.	01/10/1915	31/10/1915
Heading	49th Div Sanitary Section. Nov 1915 Vol VI		
War Diary	Nv Poperinghe	01/11/1915	30/11/1915
Heading	Summarised But Not Copied Sanitary Sect. 49th Bn. Dec Vol VII		
War Diary	Nr Poperinghe	01/12/1915	31/12/1915
Heading	49th Div Sanitary Sect Jan Vol VIII Jan 1916		
War Diary	Wormhoudt	01/01/1916	31/01/1916
Heading	49th (W. Riding) Sanitary Section Feb Mar 1916		
Miscellaneous	1/1 WR 49 Div Sanitary Sec Feb Vol 9		
War Diary	Wormhoudt	01/02/1916	03/02/1916
War Diary	Travelling	04/02/1916	04/02/1916
War Diary	Picquigny	05/02/1916	13/02/1916
War Diary	Warloy	14/02/1916	29/02/1916
Heading	49 Sanitary Section Vol X		

War Diary	Warloy	01/03/1916	03/03/1916
War Diary	Warloy Rubempre	04/03/1916	04/03/1916
War Diary	Rubempre	05/03/1916	31/03/1916
Heading	War Diary Of 49th (W.R.) Divisional Sanitary Section For The Month Of April 1916		
Heading	49 Sanitary Sect Vol XI		
War Diary	Rubempre	01/04/1916	04/04/1916
War Diary	Naours	05/04/1916	30/04/1916
Heading	49th Divl Sanitary Section May 1916		
War Diary	Naours	01/05/1916	31/05/1916
Heading	49th Divl Sanitary Section June 1916		
War Diary	Naours	01/06/1916	15/06/1916
War Diary	Naours to Val De Maison	16/06/1916	16/06/1916
War Diary	Val De Maison	17/06/1916	26/06/1916
War Diary	Rubempre	27/06/1916	30/06/1916
Heading	49th (WR) Divl Sanitary Section. July 1916		
War Diary	Val De Maison	01/07/1916	02/07/1916
War Diary	Forceville	03/07/1916	31/07/1916
Heading	49th (W.R) Divisional Sanitary Section. August 1916		
War Diary	Forceville	01/08/1916	31/08/1916
Heading	49th (W.R.) Divl San. Sect. Sept 1916		
War Diary	Forceville	01/09/1916	30/09/1916
Heading	49th Divl Sanitary Section Oct 1916		
Miscellaneous	War Diary 49 Divisional Sanitary Section Month Of October 1916		
War Diary	Couterelle	01/10/1916	21/10/1916
War Diary	Henu	22/10/1916	31/10/1916
Heading	49th Divl Sanitary Section Nov. 1916		
War Diary	Henu.	01/11/1916	30/11/1916
Heading	War Diary Of 49th (W.R.) Divisional Sanitary Section For December 1916 Vol 19		
Heading	War Diary Of For 1917		
Heading	War Diary 49th Divl Sanitary Month Of December 1916		
War Diary	Henu	01/12/1916	06/12/1916
War Diary	Lucheux	11/12/1916	31/12/1916
Heading	War Diary Of 49th Divisional Sanitary Section For January 1917 Vol 20		
Heading	War Diary Of For 1917		
Heading	War Diary 49th Divisional Sanitary Section For Month Of January 1917		
War Diary	Lucheux	01/01/1917	08/01/1917
War Diary	Bavincourt	09/01/1917	31/01/1917
Heading	War Diary Of 49th (W.R.) Divl Sanitary Section For February 1917 Vol 21		
Miscellaneous	The A.D.M.S. 49th Div.	28/02/1917	28/02/1917
War Diary	Bavincourt	01/02/1917	26/02/1917
War Diary	Lucheux	27/02/1917	28/02/1917
Heading	War Diary Of Sanitary Section 49th (W.R) Division For March 1917 Vol 22		
War Diary	Lucheux	01/03/1917	01/04/1917
War Diary	Hernicourt	02/03/1917	02/03/1917
War Diary	Pernes	03/03/1917	03/03/1917
War Diary	La Gorgue.	04/03/1917	31/03/1917

Wo/05/27901

49 Sandburg Section.

49TH DIVISION

49TH W.R. DIVL SANITARY SECN

APR 1915 - ~~DEC 1916~~
MAR 1917

To 2 ARMY

131/5609

Summarised but not copied

Sanitary Section. 49th (W.R.) Division

Vol I

AMD

121/5609
S/
Oct 1915
May

Army Form C. 2118.

1/1 R. Division SANITARY SECTION

WAR DIARY
or
INTELLIGENCE SUMMARY
(Erase heading not required.)

Instructions regarding War Diaries and Intelligence Summaries are contained in F. S. Regs., Part II. and the Staff Manual respectively. Title pages will be prepared in manuscript.

Hour, Date, Place	Summary of Events and Information	Remarks and references to Appendices
4.20 p.m. 7/4/15 YORK	Mobilized Section. Strength one Officer. Twentyfive N.C. Os and men.	H.H.
8.4.15 9.4.15 10.4.15 11.4.15 12.4.15	Time taken up in training, and equipping the men of the Section, and in obtaining Stores, as laid down in Mobilization Store Table for Sanitary Section.	OON
9.0 a.m. 13.4.15 YORK	Entrained at YORK, left Station at 9.0 a.m. arrived SOUTHAMPTON at 6.25 p.m. Obtained Medical Stores. Embarked on Steam Transport MONA'S QUEEN, and sailed at 9.0 p.m.	OON
5.45 a.m. 14.4.15 HAVRE.	Arrived 5.45 a.m. at HAVRE, disembarked 6.30 a.m. Two A.S.C. drivers reported themselves, also 30 cwt. motor lorry was handed over to me. Section billetted for night in shed on Quay. Obtained further Stores from Ordnance Depot.	OON
11.0 a.m. 15.4.15 HAVRE.	Motor lorry with one Sergt. one Private and two drivers left at 11.0 with orders to report to O.C. Motor Transport at ABBEVILLE. Section left Havre by train at 11.55 a.m.	OON

Army Form C. 2118.

WAR DIARY
of
INTELLIGENCE SUMMARY

(Erase heading not required.)

Instructions regarding War Diaries and Intelligence Summaries are contained in F. S. Regs., Part II. and the Staff Manual respectively. Title pages will be prepared in manuscript.

Hour, Date, Place	Summary of Events and Information	Remarks and references to Appendices
16.4.15.	Arrived BERGUETTE 9.30 a.m. and discontinued march at ESTAIRES arriving at 6-0 p.m. Billeted at No 7 Cleaning Hospital: medical staff fine.	ditto.
17.4.15. 18.4.15. 19.4.15. 20.4.15. 21.4.15. 22.4.15. 23.4.15. 24.4.15. 25.4.15. 26.4.15.	Remained at HERVILLE carrying out inspection of billets occupied by troops of 1/1 W.R. Division; and repair work where necessary in connection with Sanitation.	ditto.
27.4.15.	Arrived ESTAIRES visited billets in RUE Grande.	ditto.
28.4.15.	Carried out inspection of billets and spraying of same in Field Ambulances; held testing and cleaning of samples from various sources.	ditto.
May 4.15.		

WAR DIARY
or
INTELLIGENCE SUMMARY
(Erase heading not required.)

Army Form C. 2118.

Hour, Date, Place	Summary of Events and Information	Remarks and references to Appendices
May 4. 15"	Arrived at FLEURBAIX. Inspected and examined various billets; results shewing. Distances moved from VII Division Sanitary Section and emptied cess pools at headquarters garrison at Bvc. ST.MAUR.	10x.
" 5. 15"	Inspection of billets continuing; also cess pools pumped out at II Brigade Headquarters FLEURBAIX. Obtained authority for application to the numbered to H.O.C. to procure I pump for use of the Section.	10x
" 6. 15. FLEURBAIX	Nine cess pools emptied; inspection of billets; and introduced general cleansing. Depots caused by lack of garrison minerins Wells; noticed considerable erosion from dustbin precautions in certain billets in respect of pumps stoneholes, ventilation and shutery.	10x
" 7. " "	Continued inspection of billets. Sample pumps delivered from common source to pump manuronk.	10x
" 8.	Weekly report sent to Cap. R.S. Other inspection continued.	20x

Army Form C. 2118.

WAR DIARY
or
INTELLIGENCE SUMMARY
(Erase heading not required.)

Instructions regarding War Diaries and Intelligence Summaries are contained in F. S. Regs., Part II. and the Staff Manual respectively. Title pages will be prepared in manuscript.

Hour, Date, Place	Summary of Events and Information	Remarks and references to Appendices
May 9. Sunday.	Bombardment by Bartlet Guns had not long pulled up in a convenient with instructions received and moved to place proper. Unable to continue Shelling made way to fighting Infantry Brestany. Section self reformed at billet. Available Shelling Gallege. Service party and Section not required for evacuation proceeded.	10 a.m.
10 " "	Billet inspection carried out. Attend presentation of any obervations.	10 am.
11 " "	Billet inspection continued. Fatigue parties prepared to proceed to position in response.	10 am.
	Through the prompt and efficient intervention in orchestration area general state speedy Brigaden.	10 am.
12 " "	Two days inspection completed. Transmission out returned to Headquarters	10 a.m.
	much and received fortune to receive adar. Billet inspection continued.	
13 " "	Company continues. Inspection and reports received and O.C. Sir St Paul to obtain movement	10 a.m.
	Orders at Divisions H.Q. made convert on in R.E. Inspected immediately by Section & Offices q W.R. + SM. Divison and Some decline	
	Field latrines and any necessary hut which weresput by Lieut. Erisman on to	
	hoops accompany which has been maintained, extension Improvement killed in area supervised by Lieutenant, and 49th (W.R.) troops in	
	over q R.E. Divison areas forced Schindelport	

Forms/C. 2118/11.

Army Form C. 2118.

WAR DIARY
or
INTELLIGENCE SUMMARY
(Erase heading not required.)

Instructions regarding War Diaries and Intelligence Summaries are contained in F. S. Regs., Part II. and the Staff Manual respectively. Title pages will be prepared in manuscript.

Hour, Date, Place	Summary of Events and Information	Remarks and references to Appendices
14. May 1915 Zeebruik	Still occupied in improving scheme for domestic arrangements for men and in drawing up instructions which have been issued to supplement the existing proper notice, consultable amount of wet weather. Had motor cycle fitted with detachable seat to take passenger setting up crew (wounded) of recesses cases.	Stock.
22 May 1915		
23 May to 15th to Zeebruik 31 May 1915	Inspections of billets (daily) by personnel of Sanitary Sections, reports rendered daily to — hand, notice had to be taken where attention is required. Brewing open pits and incinerators fitted over by many to travel pumps and fitting a funnel a wheels laced, its liquid manure being spread upon the nearer field. With cleaning up has actually come on as well and (native parties 10 per Infantry Brigade) until first filled had completed in Zeebruik Butts for purpose [illegible]	

WAR DIARY
or
INTELLIGENCE SUMMARY

(Erase heading not required.)

Army Form C. 2118.

Instructions regarding War Diaries and Intelligence Summaries are contained in F. S. Regs., Part II. and the Staff Manual respectively. Title pages will be prepared in manuscript.

Hour, Date, Place	Summary of Events and Information	Remarks and references to Appendices
	Soup from cattle transport at Ypres, to waterer could be used no apron after storage in food rently; small billets a change of water except for Brit. Army about during later weather.	
	Enemy marine heavier in forming in several places small arms; practically all the armed at 2 man units.	
	Sweeping patrols in sections covered at ly fatigue men; removal of debris from houses carried unsteadily. Large amounts have newly unvarnished feet, and we set on post orders; heaps, and left for termous use in future. long remainders of masses observed at We several hinnderive and so civilised field.	
	Water samples from various sources of supply, and from material, moves under instrument; reported upon by O. C. Canadian Public Health Service.	

Army Form C. 2118.

WAR DIARY
or
INTELLIGENCE SUMMARY
(Erase heading not required.)

Instructions regarding War Diaries and Intelligence Summaries are contained in F. S. Regs., Part II. and the Staff Manual respectively. Title pages will be prepared in manuscript.

Hour, Date, Place	Summary of Events and Information	Remarks and references to Appendices
	Appointed a survey showing division of area occupied by troops. Mesopotamia into districts for purpose of civil administration. Each district being allotted to an area according to the appendix also a copy of orders on which civil administration is to be carried out, also reports. Gradual improvement in conditions is everywhere noted. No great need for improvement in sanitation (public) except civilians. Daily reports made on political and in regular forms. Disinfected officers' assisted by sister officers outside.	1001

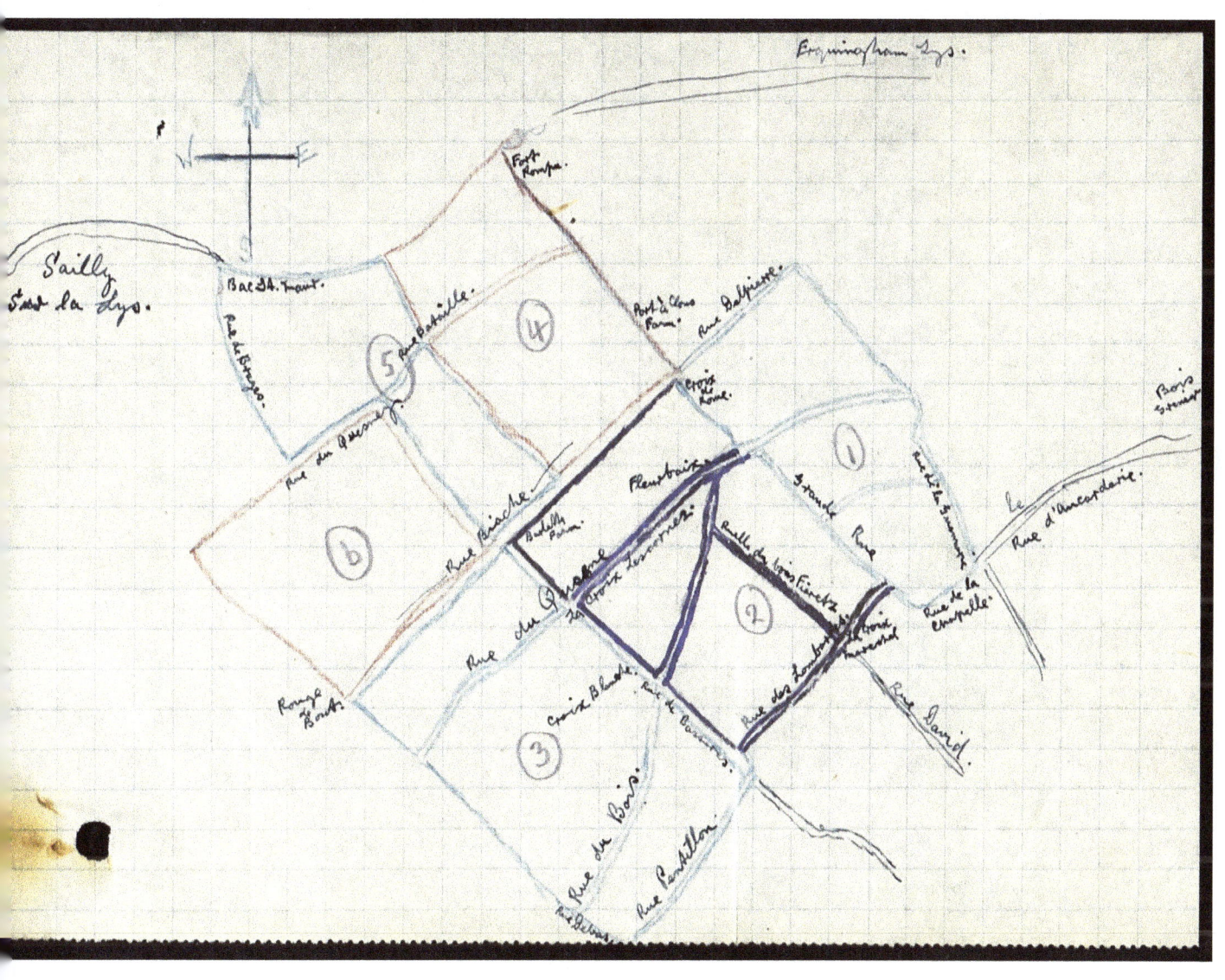

Date.

1. Name of Unit.
2. Position of Billet.
3. No. of Soldiers in Billet.
4. Number of Civilians in billet.
5. Is the Billet overcrowded.
6. Have any cases of infectious disease occurred, either in military or civil inhabitants.
7. Is there a manure heap in or near Billet?
8. If so, what treatment has been adopted to prevent flies breeding in it.
9. Are flies very numerous in the Billet?
10. Is there a cesspool or any standing water in Billet?
11. How is food stored? Is any protection for food from flies provided.
12. What is the condition of ditches near billet?
13. Is an incinerator built? If so is it working.
14. Are short trench latrines used? Are motions properly covered? Are sites of old latrines marked?
15. Is a field urine pit in use & satisfactory?
16. Are disinfectants used? State kind of disinfectant applied & quantity.
17. Where do men obtain their drinking water from?
18. What arrangements are made for washing of men in Billet?
19. Is a grease trap provided for soapy water?
20. Is debris which cannot be burnt, properly buried.
21. Are horse lines clean? Report particularly on presence or absence of flies, & also method of disposal of manure.
22. What is the condition of the latrine belonging to the civil inhabitants of Billet.
23. If a farm, state condition of cowshed, as regards cleanliness.
24. If there is a pigstye state condition.
25. If cooking is carried out in a kitchen, report on cleanliness of same.
26. Report on general cleanliness & tidiness of billet.

Dugouts to be carefully inspected & reported upon.

121/51140

49th Division.

West Riding Territorial Workshop Unit

Vol I. 10 — 30.4.15

CONFIDENTIAL

WAR DIARY

of

WEST RIDING FIELD AMBULANCE
WORKSHOP UNIT
A.S.C.

From April 10/15 to April 30/15

G E Harris
2/Lt
O.C. W. Riding F.A.W.U.

West Riding F.A.W.U.   G.S Harris 2nd Lieut

April 10th 1916

Left Grove Park London SE with complete unit. Arrived Bulford 9.30p.m.

April 11th

Drawing stores & fitting up.

April 12th

Drawing stores & fitting up.

April 13th

Drawing stores & fitting up.

April 14

Left Bulford for Avonmouth & Overseas arrived AVONMOUTH 4p.m.

April 15
Shipped ambulances in SS "Trevithoe" in charge of 1 NCO and 9 men

2.

April 16
    Left AVONMOUTH in charge of 55 men & proceeded to SOUTHAMPTON. Shipped in SS DUCHESS OF ARGYLL for ROUEN Sailed at 8.30 P.M.

April 17
    Arrived ROUEN 1.0 p.m; disembarked from SS DUCHESS OF ARGYLL. Men billeted in RIVE GAUCHE Station

April 18th
    S.S. TRAVITHOE arrived ROUEN disembarked Ambulances.
62 men inoculated for 1st time,
    055036 Pte J. ELGUERA detained in hospital.

April 19
    Received orders from ADT to proceed to ABBEVILLE.
    Inspected by ADT at 12.30 p.m.
Left ROUEN 3.30 p.m Reached NEUCHATEL 7.30 p.m Parked cars for night. Paid men of unit

3.

April 20th

Left NEUCHATEL 8.0 am. arrived ABBEVILLE 3.0 p.m. Reported to DDT received orders to proceed to MERVILLE. Parked ambulances for night.

April 21st

Left ABBEVILLE 7.0 am for MERVILLE arrived there at 3.0 p.m. reported to 4th Corps. and ADMS handed over 21 ambulances to OC's 1/1; 1/2; 1/3 West-Riding Field AMBULANCE together with 3 motor cycles. as per entry in vehicle register and attached receipts. 3 NCO's and 41 drivers as per attached receipts.
Workshop lorry; store lorry; light lorry & motor car parked at MERVILLE and temporarily attached to No 1 FIELD AMBULANCE.

April 22nd

Parked at MERVILLE

April 23

Parked at MERVILLE

4.

April 24th

    Parked at MERVILLE

April 25th

    Parked at MERVILLE

April 26th

    Parked at MERVILLE.
    Received provisional orders from A.D.M.S. W. Riding Division to be in readiness to move

April 27th

    Parked at MERVILLE
    Received orders to proceed to ESTAIRES on the 29th inst., and to be temporarily attached to 1/3 WEST RIDING FIELD AMBULANCE

April 28th

    Parked at MERVILLE.
    Reported to O/C 1/3 W Riding Field Amb. and arranged for billets.

April 29th

    Moved out of MERVILLE with Workshop Unit to ESTAIRES and billeted. left 2.10 p.m arrived 3.5 p.m

April 30th
    Parked at ESTAIRES.
    Carried out repairs etc.

131/5481

O
May 1915

49th (N.R.) Field Ambulance Workshops

Vol III

131/5481

49th (N.R.) Field Ambulance Workshops

Vol III

May 1915

CONFIDENTAL

WAR DIARY

OF

WEST RIDING FIELD AMBULANCE WORKSHOP UNIT
(ASC)

From May 1st to May 31st 1915

C.H. Harris Hall
OC W Riding FAWU

6.

May 1st/15
    Parked at ESTAIRES.
    9 men innoculated for second time.

May 2nd/15
    Parked at ESTAIRES.
    No 073376 Pte Spiller G. detained in hospital suffering from measles: (Entd: as casualty in "Roll of Co" book)

May 3rd/15
    Parked at ESTAIRES.
    9 men innoculated for second time
    Minor repairs to ambulance cars of 1/1, 1/2 & 1/3 West Riding F.A.

May 4th/15
    Parked at ESTAIRES

May 5th/15
    Parked at ESTAIRES

May 6th/1915

    Parked at ESTAIRES.
    NAPIER ambulance car for repairs cylinders cracked. Cylinders appear to be too light and not enough thickness of metal left after machining

May 7th/15

    Parked at ESTAIRES
    Inconvenience of working of unit caused by A.D.M.S. taking motor car belonging to unit, car was returned at 6 p.m.

May 8th/15

    Parked at ESTAIRES.
    Good deal of trouble with FORD AMBULANCE tyres. Tyres too small for the load put on the car, considering the overhang of the body at the back

May 9th/15

    Parked at ESTAIRES

May 10th/15

    Parked at ESTAIRES

8.

May 11/15

   Parked at ESTAIRES

May 12/15

   Parked at ESTAIRES

May 13/15

   Parked at ESTAIRES

May 14/15

   Parked at ESTAIRES

May 15/15
   P
   Parked at ESTAIRES

May 16/15

   Parked at ESTAIRES

May 17/15

   Parked at ESTAIRES

May 18/15

    Parked at ESTAIRES

May 19/15

    Parked at ESTAIRES

May 20/15

    Parked at ESTAIRES

May 21/15

    Parked at ESTAIRES

May 22/15

    Parked at ESTAIRES

May 23/15

    Parked at ESTAIRES

May 24/15

    Parked at ESTAIRES

10

May 25/15

       Parked at ESTAIRES

May 26/15

       Parked at ESTAIRES

May 27/15

       Parked at ESTAIRES

May 28/15

       Parked at ESTAIRES

May 29/15

       Parked at ESTAIRES

May 30/15

       Parked at ESTAIRES

May 31/15

       Parked at ESTAIRES

49ᵗʰ Division. Summoned but not asked

121/5992.

121/5992

49ᵗʰ Sanitary Section

Vol II

S/

June 1915.

Ans.

WAR DIARY
INTELLIGENCE SUMMARY
(Erase heading not required.)

Army Form C. 2118.

49th DIVISION SANITARY SECTION

Hour, Date, Place	Summary of Events and Information	Remarks and references to Appendices
June 1, 1915 w/ Steenwerck June 8, 1915	Inspect fine & my Sub-cleaning parties in Steenwerck continue cleaning ditches, drains, inspecting gullies & general scavenging. Latrines and steep-pit posts not practical. Emptying cesspools. We have had patrol party been kept continually employed in installing spraying gullies which case poly scour there is have occurred we disinfected & chlorinated communications at W.C.D. Gullies in back culvert trained and disinfected. Sanitary arrangements at Croonaert, de-verminizing with chlorinated large gummed? proper being also used. Have 3 men to cleaning town refuse and ordures from streets to incinerator. I shall require incinerator for street use only. Have two orderlies at Fonderies working on street cleaning and refuse removal. Inspect two civilian houses in Bue St Maur. General improvement in sanitary conditions since it came required. Water samples collected weekly and reports made received.	Appendix

WAR DIARY or INTELLIGENCE SUMMARY

Army Form C. 2118.

(Erase heading not required.)

Instructions regarding War Diaries and Intelligence Summaries are contained in F. S. Regs, Part II. and the Staff Manual respectively. Title pages will be prepared in manuscript.

Hour, Date, Place	Summary of Events and Information	Remarks and references to Appendices
June 9. 1915. FLEURBAIX	Work carried on as usual by personnel of Sanitary Section. Billet inspection. Scavenging, pumping water, cleaning etc. Scavenging fatigue parties from 2nd R.W. Surrey Regt, 1st Queens R.O.R, 1st and 2nd S.E. & Somerset Regt.: also civilian drivers not required by transport. Employment of parties of men employed by Section. Weather very hot and thundery.	100/3
June 10. 1915.	Work as usual. Personal inspection of Lieut. [?] of 3rd Byde R.F.A., Lieut [?] 9th Battery R.F.A., 5th W. Riding Regt: also civilian horses. Scavenging and working parties. Weather very hot and thundery. Shell disinfector arrived at Bac St. Maur.	100/11
June 11. 1915.	Work as usual. Personal inspection of Lieut. [?] 6th W. Yorks Regt, 2nd Lieut. [?] R.E. 3rd Byde Ammn. Column, 8 W. Yorks Regt, and No 2 Co A.S.C. and Laundries at Bac St. Maur. Scavenging and working parties. Weather cooler, rain.	100/1
June 12. 1915.	Working parties renewed interim weekly report for A.D.M.S. Fatigue civilian for work done in Sanitary Section. 2 made septic ways showing silted to latrine infectious disease received, and spraying has been carried out by personnel of Section. Scavenging and working parties. Collected various samples of mosquitoes. Accidents thermal arose for reasons that will furnish out of cesspool which deepen work of pumping party.	100/4

1247 W 3299 200,000 (E) 8/14 J.B.C. & A. Forms/C. 2118/11.

WAR DIARY
or
INTELLIGENCE SUMMARY
(Erase heading not required.)

Army Form C. 2118.

Hour, Date, Place	Summary of Events and Information	Remarks and references to Appendices
June 13. Fleurbaix	Work as usual; spraying gateways and entrances for 4th S.W. Riding Regt. Personnel inspection of men of R.A.M.C. in area in morning. River Pg's.	100¶
June 14. "	Work as usual; pumping party finished up work at Gen. Bonnet's H.Q. Two extra carts at work collecting road sweepings. Drained supervision of latrines in positions: MALLET, at RUE ST MAUR and Rue Bataille.	100¶
June 15. "	As yesterday; pumping parties; ditching; telescopic pontics, and work on 3 large incinerators in refuse field taken down; constructing engine pit for turning manure commenced. Personnel inspecting R.F.A. and R.G.A. Billets.	100¶
June 16. "	Work as usual; incinerator's being repaired and rebuilt; index grid continued; tar protection at manure. Drains repaired with D.A-159.9 billets of 6th Battery R.F.A. which were pected-opened fire has recurred in Rue Bataille; found also one Hammer manure in the billet; cut up sprays with insecticide, and on billet cleaned out ivied billets in RUE ST MAUR and FLEURBAIX	100A

WAR DIARY
or
INTELLIGENCE SUMMARY
(Erase heading not required.)

Army Form C. 2118.

Hour, Date, Place	Summary of Events and Information	Remarks and references to Appendices
June 17 FLEURBAIX.	Work as usual, personal inspection of Engineer stores & Civilian houses not occupied by troops; arranged with civilian authorities and French Mission willing to cooperate, for sanitary purposes; but exit force principally at mayors & Curates; informal arrangements impossible; intention to close & lock doors. Some field movement done.	XXX
June 18 " "	Work as usual; stores personnel working at RUE ST MAUR and me (Engineer) at FLEURBAIX; personal inspection of Engineer works, inspecting billets and on J.R.B.A. Rue Bricks; reconnaissance being pushed down in refilling; first echelon working well; grid completed and say subspecting; intersample front to trenches kilometre.	XXX
June 19 " "	Work by sections as usual; personnel weekly report; and personnel soiree E.A.S.T.S; arrived officer investigating latrines; as regards fly maggots and civilian latrines; visited latrines at RUE ST MAUR Trespinine and saw with Thad Drivepater; inspected out workings parties; Arranged with Chas. Hagmond R.E. Foxgarle; attention in opening of pumps, and cleaning of wells, which he is undertaking; will be responsible for having	XXX

WAR DIARY
or
INTELLIGENCE SUMMARY

Army Form C. 2118.

Hour, Date, Place	Summary of Events and Information	Remarks and references to Appendices
JUNE 20 FLEURBAIX	Samples of water taken from each well dealt with hypo and afli? cleaning.	
JUNE 21 " "	Personal inspection of A.S.C. and Ammunition Columns lines. Also 3rd Field Ambulance ditto. Made side phone tops had immediately with Major Murphy D.A.D.O.S. re parts, equipment, perfection etc required at once. Work found necessary, for best advantage.	
	Had a round, visited Butter of 15th R.Bat, personal inspection of N.C.O.'s & Officers. Occupied to 11 o'clock. W.H.I. interviewed. Civilians employed by Col. Haywood visited without my knowledge or reason for being so. Taken this, however matter dropt. Noted no strong movement in feed; sent a visit of Course of construction, noted killed 9/8th R.[ ]? Regt at CABOOLK MARECHAL ADAM[ ]? Group II and Caroline, Maritzini N visits laid down WSW Bois Grenier Lines, and L.M.G.	
JUNE 22 " "	Week by summer position normal. Personal visit to bombing section of 2 W 13th Infantry Brigade, reported immense debt i.e. stuff of instructors, no unantigating. Noted women civilian harvesting anyhow around husbandry scarred. Inspected billets, I Division Cyclists and L[ ]? visited from open private Harrocho, found is satisfactory.	

WAR DIARY
of
INTELLIGENCE SUMMARY
(Erase heading not required.)

Army Form C. 2118.

Instructions regarding War Diaries and Intelligence Summaries are contained in F. S. Regs., Part II. and the Staff Manual respectively. Title pages will be prepared in manuscript.

Hour, Date, Place	Summary of Events and Information	Remarks and references to Appendices
June 23. FLEURBAIX	Inspected also latrines at BUC ST MAUR; 2nd Co. R.E. BUC ST MAUR; 5th Sanitary Section transport lines and transport sheds of 5th Y. & L. Regt. also billets & shelter trenches B.4; also Regt. H.Q. B.4. W.Y. Regt. W.C.'s & urinals & men incinerators over. Work as usual: personal inspection of 1st, 5th and 5th W. Riding Regt. transport lines, 5th KOYLI and 5th Y & L transports lines at BUC ST MAUR, 10th F. Amb. Inspection of 2nd Field Ambulance lines at BUC ST MAUR. Inspection of billets. Arrangements for latrines & urinals. The grass burning. Sanitary requirements of each & environments numerously to Coln. Ins. & incinerators. Inspected EMERVILLE ward D. O. T. O. 's made to Cronwell water farmer II & 1st Canadian laboratory and water? rendering examined repaired sample. Slight showers in morning, and little or weaker noticed. Lot.	3883 / 3884
June 24. FLEURBAIX	Work as usual: inspection civilian homes and around Fleurbaix; also home lines and billets occupied by residing in FLEURBAIX.	3884
June 25. FLEURBAIX.	Work as usual: water samples taken: entrained R.E. Command re subject of pumps: inspected billets and civilian homes in BUC ST MAUR, visited LOCON with D. M. A. T. P. and HOMMS to A. A. N. of G.S.V. Division: sanitation and work in protection with Sanitary Officer 91st Division. Billets of 5th W. R. Regt & transport Scarlet Area, Henry Hendlin.	3884A

Forms/C. 2118/11

Army Form C. 2118.

WAR DIARY
or
INTELLIGENCE SUMMARY
(Erase heading not required.)

Instructions regarding War Diaries and Intelligence Summaries are contained in F. S. Regs., Part II. and the Staff Manual respectively. Title pages will be prepared in manuscript.

Hour, Date, Place	Summary of Events and Information	Remarks and references to Appendices
June 26. FLEURBAIX.	Final inspection of billets by billet-inspectors. Left FLEURBAIX at 6 p.m. and moved to DOULIEU by pm 3rd Ambulance. Weather fine.	JODM
June 27 DOULIEU.	Resting in DOULIEU. Cleaned up apparatus and everybody up there. Reinforcements from B.a.c. St MAUR to DOULIEU. Repaired motor lorry.	JODM
June 28 DOULIEU	Left DOULIEU in Evening at 8 p.m. with 10th Field Ambulance, and proceeded to MERRIS, arriving at 11.10 p.m. Weather dry showery.	JODM
June 29 MERRIS.	Left MERRIS at 7 p.m. with 10th Field Ambulance & proceeded to New PROVEN arriving at 2.15 a.m. on June 30. Heavy rain.	JODM
June 30 PROVEN.	Resting at new camp PROVEN. Cleaning up apparatus, machinery and 3 Kitchen's. Some trouble over holding phones for men and superior General Building arrangements.	JODM

Summarised but not copied

121/63m

HQrs Division

Sanitary Sect: 49th Division

Vol III

July '15

Ans

Army Form C. 2118.

WAR DIARY
of
49th DIVISION.
SANITARY SECTION.

INTELLIGENCE SUMMARY

(Erase heading not required.)

Instructions regarding War Diaries and Intelligence Summaries are contained in F. S. Regs., Part II. and the Staff Manual respectively. Title pages will be prepared in manuscript.

Hour, Date, Place	Summary of Events and Information	Remarks and references to Appendices
July 1. PROVEN.	Billet inspection, visiting and reporting on different areas; personnel to DUVIEN and supervised removal of late disinfectants up PROVEN to form. NE removed sulphuric & latrines.	dont.
July 2. PROVEN.	Billet inspection visiting billets. Latrine and cleaning selectors review. Personal inspection promises billets in neighborhood of PROVEN and ST JAN de BIEST visited and latrines will at PROVEN. Division of two PRE. to PROVEN in case of Diptheria.	dont
July 3. PROVEN.	Billet inspection working as usual. Recorded & went inspected of water supplies and testing of same and D.R.O.T.S. A Centre conference at Hrs. of SMTMI. 2 C. Corps. Inspection of billets, Sanitary work here.	dont.
July 4. 5. 6. PROVEN.	Billet inspecting as usual; personal inspection of billets near to supplies.	dont.
July 7. PROVEN.	Left PROVEN with 10th M R Bills Ambulance at 7.00 AM for Poperinghe and occupied fields near town Poperinghe - OESTON road.	dont.
8 Nr POPERINGHE.	Billet inspecting, arranging for filling apparatus for hot Pt Ambulance also research to huning hunger check.	
9" POPERINGHE to	Billet inspecting: Interior work of Sitting apparatus, selecting quite for Incinerate & others (none to Division); Inspection & purposing, inspection of billets, weeds shows and hunny shows of latrine.	dont.

Army Form C. 2118.

WAR DIARY
or
INTELLIGENCE SUMMARY

(Erase heading not required.)

Instructions regarding War Diaries and Intelligence Summaries are contained in F. S. Regs., Part II. and the Staff Manual respectively. Title pages will be prepared in manuscript.

Hour, Date, Place	Summary of Events and Information	Remarks and references to Appendices
18th July POPERINGHE	Work as usual. Three Midshipmen attached working with us spent the night under canvas.	DDN
19 July POPERINGHE	Work as usual holding forge in reserve trenches.	DDN
20 July POPERINGHE	Work as usual, incorporating dummy outpost. Waterproofs & L. supplied for Dismounted parties.	DDN DDN
21 July N. POPERINGHE	Work as usual; provided trestle aid to Division later.	DDN
22 July N. POPERINGHE	Work as usual; new nitrate furnace equipment to Camp in trenches & schools in ELVERDINGHE.	DDN
23 July N. POPERINGHE	Work as usual visit ELVERDINGHE. Went to arrange Musketry Palace Scheme with O.C. Squadron detached to 3rd Cavalry Division.	DDN
24 July N. POPERINGHE	Work as usual, visit out Q.M.S.'s & ELVERDINGHE battalion, also inspection billets & canal BURGSDINGHE — BRIELEN.	DDN
25 July N. POPERINGHE	Work as usual, visit ELVERDINGHE to see A.D.S. 1st Cavalry Division. Congratulations from Capt Copley in hospital. H.Q. appointed to Brigades Examinated at 3rd W.R.F.A. also to Brigadier's (General Group) in Squadrons in new F.T.W. heavy trenches with most as usual; wrote instructional material for B.V.	DDN
26 July N. POPERINGHE	Work in field, visit to dummy outpost replying; scheme to observe advance from Trenches & advanced Letts Resumed.	DDN

WAR DIARY
or
INTELLIGENCE SUMMARY
(Erase heading not required.)

Army Form C. 2118.

Hour, Date, Place	Summary of Events and Information	Remarks and references to Appendices
27 July. Nr POPERINGHE.	Made an immediate inspection and construction [illegible] trenches & wire entanglement from unlocated Farm below the Reninghelst-Dickebusch road, occupied by R. Reg. The Remainder were patrolled and examined by officers.	[illegible]
28 July. Nr POPERINGHE.	Wire examined; washed; received new camp for establishing Bn. exp. [illegible] morning & evening inspection BHQ; in camp; visited Divisional Amm. Col; and also Dumps W. York Regt.	[illegible]
29 July. Nr POPERINGHE.	In the morning by ranks; Reserve & Coy to Camp at ELVERDINGHE and Companies. In afternoon and evening for exercises; route march; inspection of billets new Bicycles and arranged for drawing up and erection of new trestle bridges by night — by Sunday, to ensure arrival of troops completing the [illegible]	[illegible]
30 July. Nr POPERINGHE	Made a round of posts; in morning to BRIELEN, and on to ELVERDINGHE, selected billets of Reserve & HQ billets dumped, and attended meeting dispersed. Removed Bridles, bridles kept on horses all day	[illegible]
31 July. Nr POPERINGHE.	Made usual inspection; paraded into Free hill, M.G., Reg. Bomb, and men. Reserve' Company, marches over to them; constructed trenches. Saw General messing of other companies or their exercises in musketry, grenades.	[illegible]

49th Division
summarised but not copied

1/51/7049

49th Divl: Suvla Bay sector

Vol IX

Aug & Sept. 15

S/ Sept 1915
Aug -

WAR DIARY or INTELLIGENCE SUMMARY

Army Form C. 2118.

49th DIVISION SANITARY SECTION
Lt. Stephen Capt RAMC

Hour, Date, Place	Summary of Events and Information	Remarks and references to Appendices
Aug 1 N. POPERINGHE	Improvements effected at incinerators and incinerate supplies experienced in General Latrines. Proposed latrines inspected. Inspected 247 R.E. Co's and Corps Divr. Wells on premises inspected and reported upon. Public Baths in men's homes inspected, found unsatisfactory condition. Increased Corps pay on account of washing. Sanitation of 1st N. Riding Divl Ambulance.	100A.
Aug 2 N. POPERINGHE	Inspection of Wells and ? pumping operations and disinfection of Well (civilian) in which one soldier had recovered at BRIELEN. Spraying of HQrs billets for R.K.R.F.A. Gar	100A.
Aug 3 N. POPERINGHE	Inspections and pumping operations and ? disinfection Château: and chalets this Divr.	100A.
Aug 4 N. POPERINGHE	Inspections and pumping operations and ? wells including men inspected of latrines, billets, MT, Sgts Church etc. Procured and given ?	100A.
Aug 5 N. POPERINGHE	Inspection and pumping operations around spraying of Johnston Hq and HOSPITAL FARM. Inspected Wells, water latrines, refuse pits of the Cook Huts BAVERINGHOVE etc. Permanganate Sd Co. New incinerator built.	100A.
Aug 6 N. POPERINGHE	Inspections, spraying around: approved will new pumping of Water from ditches at Huts; inspected J.A.B.C. hut, incinerators and disinfecting apparatus for of billets and reported departing arrangements.	100A.

WAR DIARY
or
INTELLIGENCE SUMMARY

(Erase heading not required.)

Army Form C. 2118.

Hour, Date, Place	Summary of Events and Information	Remarks and references to Appendices
Aug 7. M. POPERINGHE	Inspection and pumping as usual; Inspection visited by Captn Copeman and visited AYERDINGHE CHATEAU waterworks to prepare preliminary schedule there. [illegible] visit. Frenchmen were received by troops on 4/5 Div. area; installed various sources of water supply with Capt Copeman.	DOH
Aug 8. M. POPERINGHE	Inspections & pumping as usual; installed numerous wells, and some occupied by Inbenburg Bath, insect. hut cleaning & [illegible] for improvement, made repair to pumps. Effluents from piggeries very satisfactory.	DOH
Aug 9. M. POPERINGHE	Inspection & pumping as usual; insect. hut cleaning out party duty; installed numerous pits, temporary pans. Inspection with Capt Harry R.A.M.C. later no D.A.D.O. Plenty of chloride of lime; visited cavalry camp and had consultation with type supply camp; visited Div. General Division regarding sanitation & [illegible] camp. RAMC. S.a.D glendry chaleau camp. Glendryp Chaleau Camp.	DOH
Aug 10. M. POPERINGHE	Inspection and pumping as usual: visited Plenty & chaleau; consultation with troops in a boiler: [illegible] trained in 4 3rd Bgde R.F.A. Ho. Inspection [illegible] ovens & camp. Unadilla farm, and murrilled Heavy Battery.	DOH
Aug 11 M. POPERINGHE	Inspection & pumping as usual; made EXPRESSOUT Temalite unit Capt Copeman to watch water troubles: visit to battery troopers battic; and [illegible] Britton camps.	DOH

WAR DIARY
or
INTELLIGENCE SUMMARY
(Erase heading not required.)

Army Form C. 2118.

Instructions regarding War Diaries and Intelligence Summaries are contained in F. S. Regs., Part II. and the Staff Manual respectively. Title pages will be prepared in manuscript.

Hour, Date, Place	Summary of Events and Information	Remarks and references to Appendices
Aug 12. N'r Poperinghe.	O.C. Sanitary Section proceeded on leave from Aug 13 – Aug 20. Work as usual by personal of Section.	JGSH
Aug 13 – Aug 20. N'r POPERINGHE.	O.C. Section away on leave and remainder on usual Sanitary duties. Sgt Garrett also away on leave. Returned Aug 20.	JGSH
Aug 21. N'r POPERINGHE.	Took over usual inspection (rounds) of BLAREINGHE Chateau encampment; found sanitation satisfactory. Visited incinerator field, finding accumulation of rubbish in front preventing mounds of incineration; ordered this move to be built.	JGSH
Aug 22. N'r POPERINGHE.	Work as usual; incinerator building.	JGSH
Aug 23. N'r POPERINGHE.	Work as usual; personal inspection of camp lands and trenches; no evidence in defence for disposal prohibited from this area.	JGSH
Aug 24. N'r POPERINGHE.	Work as usual; personal inspection of latrines, Battns. A.S.C. lines, Mintotype men attached for duty.	JGSH
Aug 25. N'r POPERINGHE.	Work as usual; personal inspection of resting Brigade lines. No 2468 Pte Hancock W.S. from 3 London Sanitary Company arrived for duty.	JGSH

1247 W 3299 200,000 (E) 8/14 J.B.C. &A. Form C. 2118/1.

WAR DIARY
or
INTELLIGENCE SUMMARY

(Erase heading not required.)

Army Form C. 2118.

Instructions regarding War Diaries and Intelligence Summaries are contained in F. S. Regs., Part II. and the Staff Manual respectively. Title pages will be prepared in manuscript.

Hour, Date, Place	Summary of Events and Information	Remarks and references to Appendices
Aug 26. Nr POPERINGHE.	Work as usual: No 3 inverndant completed and working; standing water pumped from advanced Hills and trenches, not knowing it in advance inverndants working well; drainage pits made for keeping them going day and night.	JAYA.
Aug 27 Nr POPERINGHE	Work as usual No 4 inverndant completed and working; pumped water in flooding conditions specially advanced Hills and trenches.	JAYA.
Aug 28 Nr POPERINGHE.	Work as usual; personal inspection; inverndants specially Hills?; pumping operations in progress at advanced Hills.	JAYA.
Aug 29 Nr POPERINGHE.	Work as usual; personal inspection of Artillery Horse Lines, Le Rugt. had returned from leave.	JAYA.
Aug 30 Nr POPERINGHE.	Work as usual; personal inspection of dugouts, transport lines, and Embarking Baths. No 17 Platoon arm. M. departed on leave.	JAYA.
Aug 31 Nr POPERINGHE	Work as usual visit to ELVERDINGHE Chateau: 12 O'BRIEN. 2nd London Sanitary Company arrived probably.	JAYA.

No 2431 PITTHEER J.

Forms/C. 2118/11.

Army Form C. 2118.

WAR DIARY
or
INTELLIGENCE SUMMARY

(Erase heading not required.)

49th DIVISION SANITARY SECTION.
Officer i/c Capt RANCE

Hour, Date, Place	Summary of Events and Information	Remarks and references to Appendices
Sept 1. Nr POPERINGHE.	Work as usual: personal inspection of various billets RFA. and R.G.A. Divisional mounted field canvas. Sprinkled with lime chloride lending to disinfection. Work as usual: personal inspection of R.F.A. billets and Repository. Lime chloride on R.A.F.C. billets.	JSON.
Sept 2. Nr POPERINGHE.		JSON.
Sept 3. Nr POPERINGHE.	Work as usual: visit to canal and new advanced billets, ambulance station. Improvement in sanitary conditions very marked: disposal of refuse by burning.	JSON.
Sept 4. Nr POPERINGHE.	Work as usual: inspection Nr RENINGHE CHATEAU and other billets.	JSON.
Sept 5. Nr POPERINGHE.	Work as usual: inspection of the existing billets and surrounding farms and crops. Drainage of trenches etc. Pte RARKER returned from leave. No 1966 Pte Daniels H from 8th Batt.W.Y. who attached for fatigue duty admitted to No 10 C.C.S.	JSON.
Sept 6. Nr POPERINGHE.	Work as usual: repairing of Nos 1 & 2 incinerators: pumping in canal having dried out: large numbers of flies still requiring attention.	JSON.

Army Form C. 2118.

WAR DIARY
or
INTELLIGENCE SUMMARY
(Erase heading not required.)

Instructions regarding War Diaries and Intelligence Summaries are contained in F. S. Regs, Part II. and the Staff Manual respectively. Title pages will be prepared in manuscript.

Hour, Date, Place	Summary of Events and Information	Remarks and references to Appendices
Sept 7. Nr POPERINGHE.	Work as usual; work (photography) which arrived not many anticipated during past weeks; inspection (personal) generators, plotting boards, tripods.	JCDN.
Sept 8. Nr POPERINGHE.	Work as usual; personal inspection of pickets in vicinity of BRIELEN.	JCDN.
Sept 9. Nr POPERINGHE.	Work as usual; personal inspection of Butchery Battalion armament, A.S.C. details.	JCDN.
Sept 10. Nr POPERINGHE.	Work as usual; personal inspection of pickets in vicinity of ELVERDINGHE.	JCDN.
Sept 11. Nr POPERINGHE.	Work as usual; personal inspection of pickets (ordnance) and Canal bank.	MPH.
Sept 12. Nr POPERINGHE.	Work as usual; personal inspection of Artillery wagon lines.	JCDN.
Sept 13. Nr POPERINGHE.	Work as usual; personal inspection of pickets (various) guarding ammunition Columns.	JCDN.
Sept 13. Nr POPERINGHE.	Work as usual; personal inspection of R.E. details.	JCDN.
Sept 14. Nr POPERINGHE.	Work as usual; personal visit to ELVERDINGHE CHATEAU Camp.	JCDN.

Army Form C. 2118.

WAR DIARY
or
INTELLIGENCE SUMMARY
(Erase heading not required.)

Instructions regarding War Diaries and Intelligence Summaries are contained in F. S. Regs., Part II. and the Staff Manual respectively. Title pages will be prepared in manuscript.

Hour, Date, Place	Summary of Events and Information	Remarks and references to Appendices
Sept 15 Nr POPERINGHE.	Work as usual; visit to Brigade Transport Lines and afternoon hockey.	JOOA.
Sept 16 Nr POPERINGHE.	Work as usual; personal inspection of 145th Infantry Brigade.	JOOA.
Sept 17 Nr POPERINGHE.	Work as usual; spare in pauseo of Artillery lines – new Farm Dimps. and BEISLEN.	JOOA.
Sept 18 Nr POPERINGHE.	Work as usual; personal inspection of lines in Camp Bouds. No 5/1 Pte Tepand J. remanded to Bond. [Dulverhope no permanently unfit]. No 2902 Pte South E.W. Yorks Regt. attached to fatigue duties evacuated our personnel area.	
Sept 19 Nr POPERINGHE.	Work as usual; personal inspection of arrangements in accepted field and smelter firstimple refuse destructor, now erected by Infantry Brigade Relief.	JOOA.
Sept 20 Nr POPERINGHE.	Work as usual; personal inspection accompanying Regt. lines in area.	JOOA.
Sept 21 Nr POPERINGHE.	Work as usual; personal inspection of R.E. billets, and of supply column.	JOOA.

WAR DIARY
or
INTELLIGENCE SUMMARY
(Erase heading not required.)

Army Form C. 2118.

Hour, Date, Place	Summary of Events and Information	Remarks and references to Appendices
Sept 22 Nr POPERINGHE.	Work as usual. Twenty two footype mines dumped for attachment to ditch cleaning machine; escort to Experimental Farm/field.	JOSN.
Sept 23 Nr POPERINGHE.	Work as usual. Ditch cleaning [illegible] Wormhoudt under supervision. Ground work [illegible] Bullet camp.	JOSN.
Sept 24 Nr POPERINGHE.	Work as usual; received return German footype mines from units.	JOSN.
Sept 25 Nr POPERINGHE.	Work as usual; [illegible] investigation under repair sent to Proven for washing. Circle accommodation held [illegible], not free units' billets.	JOSN.
Sept 26 Nr POPERINGHE.	Work as usual; visit to [illegible] Supports, Bullet Hill.	JOSN.
Sept 27 Nr POPERINGHE.	Work as usual; visit to ELVERDINGHE & H.Q. CHATEAU AREA.	JOSN.
Sept 28 Nr POPERINGHE.	Work as usual; visit to Advanced billets, Y.R.F.A.	JOSN.
Sept 29 Nr POPERINGHE.	Work as usual; general inspection of jumping huts, [illegible] area. Footype men sent to Wormhoudt for ditch cleaning.	JOSN.

Army Form C. 2118.

WAR DIARY
or
INTELLIGENCE SUMMARY

(Erase heading not required.)

Hour, Date, Place	Summary of Events and Information	Remarks and references to Appendices
Sept 30 nr POPERINGHE.	Made no remark; did the cleaning posts: no work showing pants lest sur did the death roll in a month.	Adam.

121/7333

4th Bn Khotan
summoned but not acted

Oct 15

49th Sanitary Section
Pt II

Oct 15

Army Form C. 2118.

WAR DIARY
or
INTELLIGENCE SUMMARY
49th Division SANITARY SECTION.

(Erase heading not required.)

W. Offord Captain

Hour, Date, Place	Summary of Events and Information	Remarks and references to Appendices
Oct 1. N° POPERINGHE.	Work as usual; whilst cleaning forks at work; and Pte Crook Bruce.	JSON
Oct 2. N° POPERINGHE.	Letters sent to R§A billet at ELVERDINGHE. Work as usual; visited incinerator pits; improvement of sanitation; erection & exhibition of sanitary appliances invited. Pte was introduced. Visited D.D.M.S. 6th Corps Office for evidence.	JSON
Oct 3. N° POPERINGHE.	Work as usual; personal inspection of personnel billets and sanitary arrangements being made.	JSON
Oct 4. N° POPERINGHE.	Work as usual; visited Divisional Field Pk Clarke returned from leave today; personal inspection of Resting Brigade. Arrangements for personal inspection of 147th Infantry Brigade at RANGE STAFF.	JSON
Oct 5. N° POPERINGHE.	Work as usual; personal inspection of 147th Infantry Brigade within RANGE STAFF. Sgt F Clarke returned (school) from Rouen.	JSON
Oct 6. N° POPERINGHE.	Work as usual; personal inspection of Artillery arrangements and transport lines of 146th Brigade.	JSON
Oct 7. N° POPERINGHE.	Work as usual; personal inspection of Scouting Battalions, and camp HQ in.	JSON
Oct 8 N° POPERINGHE.	Work as usual; personal inspection of MILL MERKEMHOEK CHATEAU B.De/ELEN, and canal bank accommodations.	JSON

1247 W 3299 200,000 (E) 8/14 J.B.C. & A. Forms/C. 2118/11.

Army Form C. 2118.

WAR DIARY
or
INTELLIGENCE SUMMARY
(Erase heading not required.)

Instructions regarding War Diaries and Intelligence Summaries are contained in F. S. Regs., Part II. and the Staff Manual respectively. Title pages will be prepared in manuscript.

Hour, Date, Place	Summary of Events and Information	Remarks and references to Appendices
Oct 9. Nr POPERINGHE.	Work as usual; visits to Divisionate field inspection of ammunition columns.	WJA.
Oct 10 Nr POPERINGHE.	Work as usual; visit to Artillery lines; lents of 2nd Lieut Z. RE Lewis and hands of Yr Baillie R.F.A. also 107th Batty R.F.A.	WJA.
Oct 10 — Oct 26 Nr POPERINGHE	Work as usual, daily inspection of lines.	WJA.
Oct 27 Nr POPERINGHE.	Capt. H. F. HORNE evacuated sick, and Capt ADAMSON. W. W. took over work of the unit.	WJA.
Oct 28 Nr POPERINGHE.	Work as usual. Inspection of gun pillbox.	WJA.
Oct 29. Nr POPERINGHE	Work as usual. Personal inspection of drains at Headquarters 3rd Bde R.F.A. Raining.	WJA.
Oct 30. Nr POPERINGHE.	Work as usual. Inspection of ammo lorries. Dry.	WJA.
Oct 31. Nr POPERINGHE.	Work as usual. Dry.	WJA.

S

Nov 1/15

Summarised but not actic'd

12/
7637

to Pol. Secretary Sec..

Noted. R.S.

VI
10/

WAR DIARY
or
INTELLIGENCE SUMMARY

Army Form C. 2118.

49th W.R. Sanitary Section

(Erase heading not required.)

Instructions regarding War Diaries and Intelligence Summaries are contained in F. S. Regs., Part II. and the Staff Manual respectively. Title pages will be prepared in manuscript.

Hour, Date, Place		Summary of Events and Information	Remarks and references to Appendices
November 1st	Nr. POPERINGHE	Work as usual. Inspection of fields	W.H.A.
Nov. 2nd	Nr. POPERINGHE	Work as usual.	W.H.A.
Nov. 3rd	Nr. POPERINGHE	Work as usual. Received report of upper lip bullet of 4th W.R. RFA Bde BATTERY and 6th BATTERY. R.F.A.	W.H.A.
Nov. 4th	Nr. POPERINGHE	Work as usual. NO. 11. PTE. BROWN. S.C. rejoined section from leave	W.H.A.
Nov. 5th	Nr. POPERINGHE	Removed Sanitary section to fresh site. A. 23. a. 8. 4. Sheet 28 N.W.	W.H.A.
Nov. 6	Nr. POPERINGHE	Began erecting bridge to site of new incinerator field A. 18. c. 5. 3.	W.H.A.
Nov. 7	Nr. POPERINGHE	Work as usual.	W.H.A.
Nov. 8	Nr. POPERINGHE	Work as usual.	W.H.A.
Nov. 9	Nr. POPERINGHE	Work as usual. STAFF. SQT. MORRELL proceeded to England on report to War Office.	W.H.A.
Nov. 10	Nr. POPERINGHE	Work no usual.	W.H.A.
Nov. 11	Nr. POPERINGHE	Work as usual. Started work burning rubbish in new incinerator field	W.H.A.
Nov. 12	Nr. POPERINGHE	Work as usual	W.H.A.
Nov. 13	Nr. POPERINGHE	Work as usual	W.H.A.
Nov. 14	Nr. POPERINGHE	Work as usual	W.H.A.
Nov. 15	Nr. POPERINGHE	Work as usual. Received post 6 7. W.R. Regt. on parties to 9th BATTERY. R.F.A.	W.H.A.

WAR DIARY
or
INTELLIGENCE SUMMARY
(Erase heading not required.)

Army Form C. 2118.

Hour, Date, Place	Summary of Events and Information	Remarks and references to Appendices
Nov. 16. N^r POPERINGHE	} Intake usual.	WNA.
Nov. 17. N^r POPERINGHE		WNA.
Nov. 18. N^r POPERIJNGHE		WNA.
Nov. 19. N^r POPERINGHE	Intake as usual. Personal inspection of 7th W.R. Regt. wagon line.	WNA.
Nov. 20. N^r POPERINGHE	Intake usual.	WNA.
Nov. 21. N^r POPERINGHE	Intake usual. Personal inspection of 4th KOYLI Regt. line.	WNA.
Nov. 22. N^r POPERINGHE	Intake usual. Personal inspection of wagon lines of 5th W.R. REGT, 6th W.R. REGT, 7th W.R. REGT. Wagon lines of 9th BATTERY R.F.A.	WNA.
Nov. 23. N^r POPERINGHE	Intake usual. Personal inspection of wagon lines of NORTH RIDING SEIGE BATTERY. Situated on main Poperinghe road at WOESTE - PESELHOEK Road. A. 16. a. 7. 6.	WNA.
Nov. 24. N^r POPERINGHE	Intake usual. Ditches being cleaned out.	WNA.
Nov. 25. N^r POPERINGHE	Intake usual. Personal inspection of 4th YORK and LANCASTER REGT - HEADQUARTERS — with its Rest Camp. wagon lines as usual. Provided with wireless circumnutator pole.	WNA.
Nov. 26. N^r POPERINGHE	Intake usual. Snow showers.	WNA.
Nov. 27. N^r POPERINGHE	Intake usual. Hard-Frost. Personal inspection of 57th FIELD. CO. R.E. billets	WNA.

WAR DIARY
or
INTELLIGENCE SUMMARY

(Erase heading not required.)

Army Form C. 2118.

Hour, Date, Place	Summary of Events and Information	Remarks and references to Appendices
Nov. 28. Nr POPERINGHE	Work as usual. Billet inspection as usual. Reconnaissance parties made stopped as the several workparties and teams first, the final two tires. Personnel outposts of no. 2 REST CAMP which we occupied h/K also inspecting workparties of 7th WEST YORK REGT. 5th WEST YORK 6th WEST YORK } REGT. 7th WEST YORK.	W.D.A.
Nov. 29 Nr POPERINGHE	Work as middleting + inspections as usual. Went to C.R.E. to draw money for paying workparties employed for Reconnaissance of trenches of NORTH RIDING HEAVY BATTERY - improvements to lines trench also of the NORTH MIDLAND BATTERY and the DIVISIONAL CYCLIST CO.	W.D.A.
Nov. 30. Nr POPERINGHE.	Inspection of billets as usual as usual. Reconnaissance of trenches by workparties about of 10th + 3rd MONMOUTHS. REGT. - a new workparty camp. the 7th ENTRENCHING BATTALION and ENTRENCHING BATTALION - it Later November from line transitory found 4 vol Roman inspection of 2/1st W.R. FLD. Co. R.E. Remarks for two sanitary arrangements both moved to new in various fields.	W.D.A.

Investigated but not acted
Sanitary Secs. 49th Dn.
Dec
vol. VII

J.S.

Dec 1915

Army Form C. 2118.

WAR DIARY
or
INTELLIGENCE SUMMARY

49th (W.R.) Division — Sanitary Section

(Erase heading not required.)

Hour, Date, Place	Summary of Events and Information	Remarks and references to Appendices
Dec 1st Nr POPERINGHE	Weather variable. Billet inspection as carried arms round. Personal inspection of Quartermaster Stores of 6th WEST RIDING REGT. and also wagon lines of H.Q., 1st W.R. Bde. R.F.A. and wagon lines of H.Q. Divisional R.F.A. also 1/2nd W.R. FLD. CO. R.E. lines. New Incinerator Field A.16, a.7-b. Hut 28. N.W. is now ready for working out dustings etc. refuse from units adjoining to PESELHOEK – WOESTON Road.	W.A.
Dec 2nd Nr POPERINGHE	Billet inspection and general work as usual. Visited First Incinerator Field	W.A.
Dec 3rd Nr POPERINGHE	Work as usual. Personal inspection of H.Q. of 5th K.O.Y.L.I. + no. 1 REST CAMP. also of 2/1 FLD. CO. R.E. – Visited Second Incinerator field on POPERINGHE – WOESTON Road. Motor Lorry – broken down turned to PROVAN Bye fair. New Incinerator field started working. Wet day.	W.A.
Dec 4th Nr POPERINGHE	Personal inspection of 4th YORK + LANCASTER. and 5th YORK + LANCASTER. and wagon lines. Motor Lorry still out. Very stormy at night.	W.A.
Dec 5th Nr POPERINGHE.	Work as usual. Personal inspection of 4th KOYLI. + 5th KOYLI. Large lines. Motor Lorry back. Still at work on new incinerator field improving it.	W.A.
Dec 6th Nr POPERINGHE	Work + Billet Inspection as usual. Personal inspection of 7th BATTERY. R.F.A. C/ Second Incinerator Field. Very little rubbish. Conveyed to railway field the ground.	W.A.

1247 W 3299 200,000 (E) 8/14 J.B.C. & A. Forms/C. 2118/11.

WAR DIARY
or
INTELLIGENCE SUMMARY

Army Form C. 2118.

(Erase heading not required.)

Hour, Date, Place	Summary of Events and Information	Remarks and references to Appendices
Dec 7th Nr POPERINGHE	Visiting Billets and Roads to same. Statching party worked on the POPERINGHE - WOESTON Road. Personal inspection of billets of H.Q. 33rd R.G.A.	W.D.A.
Dec 8th Nr POPERINGHE	2/1st FLD. Co. R.E. also of Q.M. store of 6 W.Y. Regt. and men of lines of 2nd BATTERY. R.F.A. Visited hospitsinster field on POPERINGHE - WOESTON Road. Pumping engines & visited billets as usual. Motor Lotine, whitenkiich, twice put inated at Technical School, B. 9. a. sheet 28 N.W. Personal inspection of AMMUNITION COL. 1st W.R. R.F.A. lines. Craftsmen lived to a demonstration on GAS ATTACK. Precautions &c	W.D.A.
Dec 9th Nr POPERINGHE	Visited 1st & 10th ENTRENCHING BATTS. Letter of when his fire in a farm which were totally destroyed. Visited Pulverisator field in POPERINGHE - ELVERDINGHE Road. Work visiting billets as usual.	W.D.A.
Dec 10th Nr POPERINGHE	Visited H.Q. St Sulg &c. & saw A.D.M.S. & A.P.M. 2nd Lieutenant went to 1st Corps H.Q. & their away at H.Q. Routing inspections to billets in hospitalar as usual.	W.D.A.
Dec 11th Nr POPERINGHE	Personal Inspection of H.Q. of R.F.A. (W.R.) also visited AMMUNITION COL. 4th (HOW) BDE R.F.A. horse lines on the Pulverisator Field in POPERINGHE - WOESTON Rd. Billets inspections as usual. Located at BREWERY, ELVERDINGHE. Summit.	W.D.A.
Dec 12th Nr POPERINGHE	Personal Inspection of Billets of DIVISIONAL MINING SECTION and TRENCH MORTAR SECTION and were Coy of 4th BATTERY R.F.A. Billet inspections as usual also visited 1st pulverisator field on ELVERDINGHE Rd. DEAD HORSE buried at Cross Roads - BRIELEN	W.D.A.

WAR DIARY or INTELLIGENCE SUMMARY

Army Form C. 2118.

Hour, Date, Place	Summary of Events and Information	Remarks and references to Appendices
Dec. 13th Nr POPERINGHE	Visited Bath marquee. Talked with the D.A.D.M.S. about the WINDMILL DUMP. Carpet fitter at 8.1 Battery WAGM. Bivouacs being built down and men moved into tents. Shed has been erected. Also visited BATHS.	W.S.A.
Dec. 14th Nr POPERINGHE	Personal Inspection of 33rd R.G.A. H.Qrs. also of 3rd MON:MOUTH. magazines finished the letters having just moved. Weekly ditch at ARGYLE wagon lines. A.S.C. kills Nos 1 & 2 Companies. Bivouacs very nearly done. Otherwise normal. The A.S.C. at Brielen came into No 2 REST CAMP and SUTHERLAND Hy. at of M.R. AMMUNITION COL. and damp visited it.	W.S.A.
Dec. 15th Nr POPERINGHE	Personal Inspection of the YORK & LANC. REGT had just come into billets at the A.S.C. billets which it took over the ditch within within ditches Incinerator field on WOESTON ROAD. Billets Inspections as normal. and also pumping Carports at BRIELEN.	W.S.A.
Dec. 16th Nr POPERINGHE	Personal Inspection of WINDMILL DUMP and visited Incinerator on Slaughter Rd. also visited 2nd Bde AMMUNITION R.F.A. billets and EXPEDITIONARY FORCE CANTEEN. working ditch at A.S.C. Billets & also Inspected Carports at BRIELEN & A.S.C. billets	W.S.A.
Dec. 17th Nr POPERINGHE	W.N. normal. Still working & ditches. Billet Inspections normal.	W.S.A.
Dec. 18th Nr POPERINGHE	work as usual. working on ditches at A.S.C. billets of 5th & 6th & 7th 8th WEST YORKSHIRE Personal Inspection of P.M. store of Incinerator field on WOESTON – OESELHOEK Road. REGT. visited	W.S.A.

WAR DIARY
or
INTELLIGENCE SUMMARY

(Erase heading not required.)

Army Form C. 2118.

Instructions regarding War Diaries and Intelligence Summaries are contained in F. S. Regs, Part II. and the Staff Manual respectively. Title pages will be prepared in manuscript.

Hour, Date, Place	Summary of Events and Information	Remarks and references to Appendices
Dec. 19th N. POPERINGHE	GAS ATTACK on our trenches by GERMANS. Men kept ready to attend to MOTOR LORRY and to take slightly wounded cases & slight cases of GASSED men to No. 17. C.C.S. at POPERINGHE. 24 cases were wounded by the Envy. Also 58 patients who were in the Field Ambulance (No. 2 WEST RIDING FLD. AMB.) were cleared to the DIVISIONAL REST STATION on the WOESTEN-PESIELHOEK ROAD. All the men had their Gas helmets inspected at the encampment. Laminator fields working as usual. The services of CAPT ADAMSON O.C. 1/c SAN. SECTION placed at disposal of COL. COLLINSON O.C. 2" W.R. FLD. AMBULANCE. Ditching party at work in Brigadier of 5" BATTERY RFA.	W.W.A.
Dec. 20th N. POPERINGHE	All working parties out as usual. Ditching party at WINDMILL DUMP. Visited Inmates field in POPERINGHE-ELVERDINGHE Road & procured expected billets of 10th ENTRENCHING BATT. Cesspool emptied at waggon-line of 2nd BATTERY. R.F.A. MOTOR LORRY no straight transit slightly wounded & gassed cases from ESSEX FARM.	W.W.A.
Dec. 21st N. POPERINGHE	Work as usual. Visited Inoculation field in PESELHOEK-WOESTEN Road. Parcel inspection of billets of BATTERY. TRENCH MORTAR & 2m BDE. AMMUN. COL. R.F.A. Ditching party at A.S.C. billet	W.W.A.
Dec. 22nd N. POPERINGHE	Work as usual. Ditti party to A.S.C. billet. Visited Inoculation field on ELVERDINGHE-POPERINGHE Road. Trench grids laid down all over camp.	W.W.A.

Army Form C. 2118.

WAR DIARY
or
INTELLIGENCE SUMMARY
(Erase heading not required.)

Instructions regarding War Diaries and Intelligence Summaries are contained in F. S. Regs., Part II. and the Staff Manual respectively. Title pages will be prepared in manuscript.

Hour, Date, Place	Summary of Events and Information	Remarks and references to Appendices
Dec 23rd Nr POPERINGHE	Personal Inspection of Billets of ARGYLL & SUTHERLAND HIGHLANDERS 9th Batt. — at CHATEAU DE TROIS TOURS. also of billets of 7th SIEGE BATTERY. R.G.A. visited billets in POPERINGHE — ELVERDINGHE Road. Arrangements	WWA
Dec 24th Nr POPERINGHE	Work regimental. Cleaned out ditch at 9th BATTERY. R.F.A. Inspected troops camped & 8th BATTERY R.F.A. lines. visited A.D.M.S. to see about billets in area where lines in grounds met.	WWA
Dec 25th Nr POPERINGHE	Christmas Day. Went with Staff Capt. to find a billet for the section at WORMHOUDT. Unsuccessful in their endeavour.	WWA
Dec 26th Nr POPERINGHE	Visited STE SIXTE tree A.D.M.S. Investigated a Case of SCARLET FEVER at 1st ENTRENCHING BATT. & had a hut & tent sprayed with formalin. Visited divisional field in POPERINGHE – ELVERDINGHE Road.	WWA

WAR DIARY
or
INTELLIGENCE SUMMARY

(Erase heading not required.)

Army Form C. 2118.

Hour, Date, Place	Summary of Events and Information	Remarks and references to Appendices
Dec 27. Nr POPERINGHE.	Visited Divisional field & ELVERDINGHE – POPERINGHE Road & Runnell inspected Q.M. Stores of 7th W.R. Regt. visited Divisional field on WOESTEN – PIESELHOEK Road. Billet Inspection as usual.	WMA
Dec. 28. Nr POPERINGHE.	Went to WORMHOUDT to look for billets for this section but unsuccessful. All fatigue men of 148th BRIGADE sent back to their units. Billets allotted to the unit.	WMA
Dec. 29. Nr POPERINGHE.	Visited Divisional fields & other parts of Div. area. All men of 146th BRIGADE & Division who take over from us sent back to their units. Sam. Officer of 14th Division remainder on fatigue duty.	WMA
Dec. 30. Nr POPERINGHE.	Began moving the idler. Sent a party to clean men of the billets & part of Stores sent also. Section put on the Divisional fields. Visited 1st ENTRENCHING BATTALION & found all satisfactory. So isolated men who had been in contact with the SCARLET FEVER case were taken out & sent back to duty.	WMA

1247 W 3299 200,000 (E) 8/14 J.B.C. & A.   Forms/C. 2118/11.

Army Form C. 2118.

WAR DIARY
or
INTELLIGENCE SUMMARY
(Erase heading not required.)

Instructions regarding War Diaries and Intelligence Summaries are contained in F. S. Regs., Part II. and the Staff Manual respectively. Title pages will be prepared in manuscript.

Hour, Date, Place	Summary of Events and Information	Remarks and references to Appendices
Dec 31st Nr POPERINGHE	Cleaning up camp & disposal of last of refuse at both Incinerator fields. Removed to new Billets at WORMHOUDT — C.17.c.1-5. Sheet 27. — Leaving fatigue party behind to clean up the Camp.	W.J.A.

1247 W 3290 200,000 (E) 8/14 J.B.C. & A.   Forms/C. 2118/1L.

49th Div Sanitary Sect

Som

Vol VIII

F/2661

Jan 1916

Army Form C. 2118.

WAR DIARY
or
INTELLIGENCE SUMMARY
(Erase heading not required.)

49th Divisional Sanitary Section (West Riding).

Instructions regarding War Diaries and Intelligence Summaries are contained in F. S. Regs., Part II. and the Staff Manual respectively. Title pages will be prepared in manuscript.

Hour, Date, Place	Summary of Events and Information	Remarks and references to Appendices
January 1st WORMHOUDT.	Finished all moving fixtures etc. from previous camp. Cleaning up and left - state from in charge of it. General cleaning up.	W.T.A.
Jan. 2nd WORMHOUDT.	Put up latrines marking place where sanitary conveniences for the unit. Visited 146th Bde. H.Q. to find out position of farms units. Examined reported an water supply of area occupied by unit.	W.T.A.
Jan 3rd WORMHOUDT.	Visited H.Q. & billets of 3rd MONMOUTHS. Still working on sanitary arrangement of billets & latrines. Sprayed out pail system occupied by men suffering from SCABIES.	W.T.A.
Jan 4th WORMHOUDT.	Inspected H.Q. 1st BDE. R.F.A. at ZEGGERS-CAPPEL. Started lectures on First Aid work to men of section who move about in charge of gas when the Division is in trenches. Strong wind.	W.T.A.
Jan 5th WORMHOUDT.	Inspected H.Q. of YORKSHIRE HUSSARS at DEN NAGTEGHEL. Made various arrangements as to loan of bicycles for billet inspectors who have large area to work in. Examined form of sanitary and sanitary inspection. Strong wind.	W.T.A.
Jan 6th WORMHOUDT.	Drew 4 bicycles from store at POPERINGHE which we got on loan from the Cyclist Co. Personal inspection of MOTOR MACHINE GUN CO. at WATOU and also visited H.Q. of 4th WEST RIDING REGT at HOUDT KERQUE. Weather finer day with strong winds.	W.T.A.

WAR DIARY
or
INTELLIGENCE SUMMARY

Army Form C. 2118.

(Erase heading not required.)

Hour, Date, Place	Summary of Events and Information	Remarks and references to Appendices
Jan. 7th. WORMHOUDT.	Visited ESQUELBECQ to see about FODEN LORRY with Disinfector — then this afternoon. 4 billet inspection started at Dunk — then trip to allen occupied by ARTILLERY's one billet to HERZEELE + one to WINNEZEELE. Personal Inspection of billets of DIVISIONAL MINING CO. at J.9. Sheet 27 N.E.	W.W.W.
Jan. 8th. WORMHOUDT	Lecture on First Aid. Personal Inspection of TRENCH MORTAR BATTERY at ZEGGERS-CAPPEL — found the Sanitary arrangements + billets very fairly satisfactory. The FODEN LORRY + THRESH DISINFECTOR arrived late in afternoon from the 14th DIVISION BATHS. The YORKSHIRE HUSSARS are being visited by a Sanitary Corporal each day for 3 days to supervise a team of pioneers for their sanitary work.	W.W.W.
Jan 9th. WORMHOUDT	Started work with THRESH DISINFECTOR + stoved 744 blankets +. After preliminaries + trifling delays the first day, each blanket went 45 minutes for disinfection. Arrangements were made to deal with the whole of the 146th BDE no regards blankets + dirty shirts in the next 3 days, one battalion having been finished with today. YORKSHIRE HUSSARS visited and found the Sanitary arrangements improved. At one farm the water was frightening, had a considerable amount of contamination. A 9 ft ground sheet it should be removed for another one. The pump (inside the house) should be now instead. Billets of the 3 farms into all satisfactory. Billet refused occupied by J.S. W.YORKS at C.10 a. Sh.8. here had water depth — from a contaminated pond + cess of disorderliness there.	W.W.W.

WAR DIARY
or
INTELLIGENCE SUMMARY
(Erase heading not required.)

Army Form C. 2118.

Hour, Date, Place	Summary of Events and Information	Remarks and references to Appendices
January 10th WORMHOUDT	Billet Inspection is moved — C. Company, 5th W.Y. & their Transport Vehicles. It that which was found to unfit for billets in 5 condition at the time. 14th BDE — dirty clothing disinfected previous to their DUMP.	4.W.Y.
Jan 11th WORMHOUDT	Billet Inspector of 6 W.Y. at GRAND HOTEL WORMHOUDT — where their Linos were insanitary. SUMP PIT in the Yard. Their M.O. informed DDT.	6.W.Y.
Jan 12th WORMHOUDT	A public urinal situated against the PARISH CHURCH, WORMHOUDT here is very insanitary + the urine was flowing down the main street from it. It was cleaned out + repaired + disinfected so that it was again fit for use. Thus, though the public mind is very deeply roused by the troops, D.D.M.S. 2nd ARMY visited the SANITARY SECTION and inspected the FODEN LORRY + DISINFECTOR. Several cases of DIPTHERIA have appeared in LEDRINGHAM among the civilians. The place is put out of bounds for all troops, and the attempt to being dealt with by the Civil authorities. In this are the DIVISIONAL TRAIN A.S.C. H.Q. + no.2 Coy. were killed + they have to remove it. no.1. adult cases among the Civilians = 3. no.1. suspicious case — Our suspicious cases have been moved.	6.W.Y.

WAR DIARY
INTELLIGENCE SUMMARY

Army Form C. 2118.

Hour, Date, Place	Summary of Events and Information	Remarks and references to Appendices
Jan 13" WORMHOUDT	Billet Requisites & disinfectors of clothing etc being carried on as usual.	W.S.A.
Jan 14" WORMHOUDT	2 rooms of collection of refuse being dealt with, visited - in RUE DU PROGRES (C.5 a. 5-8) Sheet 27, & also at P.O. opposite the SANITARY SECTION. Disinfector station for 147" BDE BOMP.	W.S.A.
Jan 15" WORMHOUDT	Arranging about cleaning up ESQUELBECQ streets - to be done by prisoners under superintendence of a corporal of the SANITARY SECTION.	W.S.A.
Jan 16" WORMHOUDT	The above arrangement was illness re street cleaning at ESQUELBECQ - the Cyclist Co. being responsible. MOTOR LORRY used to take Sick men from the 2" W.R.F.Amb to MERCKEGHEM. Inspection by Col. Collinson.	W.S.A.
Jan 17" WORMHOUDT	MOTOR LORRY again used to take Sick men to STAENEEKE. Billet Inspection & disinfection also Disinfection.	W.S.A.
Jan 18" WORMHOUDT	Billet Inspection & Disinfection as before.	W.S.A.

WAR DIARY
or
INTELLIGENCE SUMMARY

(Erase heading not required.)

Army Form C. 2118.

Hour, Date, Place	Summary of Events and Information	Remarks and references to Appendices
	Return of FODEN LORRY — THRESH DISINFECTOR for the past 10 days.	
	3 hrs has been used for sack disinfection — being the time required to disinfect & to harn [hang] empty 2 electric warmers up full. 60 blankets every 1½ & complete disinfection was the result.	
	It was estimated on the first day that with this amount of time it would be possible to disinfect about 800 blankets each day working from 9 a.m. to 5 p.m. continuously.	
	At the end of this period of 10 days we found that there was such a much work to many [too many] articles has to be disinfected that it was tried to increase the no. particles placed in the disinfector each time known was found apt to work satisfactorily — no articles were not sterilised satisfactorily & has it be resterilised	G.W.A.

The causes for this were more than one —

1st the greater no. of vehicles in the columns at the ourset[?] [one word].

2nd the articles have sometimes not therefore needed a longer period [insufficient?];

3rd the water used in the Boilers was not of good quality & perhaps has caused a certain amount of deposit on the Boilers.

4th the poor type of coal supplied rendered it difficult to keep the steam up to the required pressure;

It is therefore advisable to always cut down the number of articles standing for say 3 to 500 Kandats (B shirts - roats being redrawn)
As in Genenet[?].

WAR DIARY
INTELLIGENCE SUMMARY
(Erase heading not required.)

Army Form C. 2118.

Hour, Date, Place	Summary of Events and Information	Remarks and references to Appendices
Jan 19th WORMHOUDT	Visited P.O. & saw that returns left by fatigues were being cleaned up. Prepared report of FODEN LORRY → DISINFECTOR (for which see previous sheet)	W.A.F.
Jan 20 WORMHOUDT	Visited W. Riding Regt Billets, the canteen arrangements of which have improved greatly as regards mine feet. Visited terms — about various movements re Foden Lorry etc.	W.A.F.
Jan 21 WORMHOUDT	Visited large slaughter house left by 6th DIVISION — which is mostly their SUPPLY COLUMN to deport their rubbish in. Walked round it and see it on a source of great in the edge of town as unhealthy times. Put in memo to be sure that it really was the SUPPLY COLUMN who deported their. Saw floor of a slaughter house in ESQUELBEC running through the town — visited place where BATHS are contemplated for BRIGADE in ESQUELBEC. Inspecting so cannot get into French in	W.A.F.

WAR DIARY
or
INTELLIGENCE SUMMARY

Army Form C. 2118.

Hour, Date, Place	Summary of Events and Information	Remarks and references to Appendices
Jan. 21ˢᵗ WORMHOUDT.	Had definite evidence that the 6ᵗʰ DIV. SUPPLY. COL. depended on trade pullock at refuse heap mentioned above. Reported — can Slaughter house refuse to above to ADMS. Visited A.V.C. section (M.V.C.) near LEDRINGHAM. Sanitary arrangements good on the whole. BOILER inspection done — whole day in consequence no disinfection done.	W.W.A.
Jan. 22ⁿᵈ WORMHOUDT.	Reported the refuse heap to ADMS with particulars — he will take action. Visited 7. W. RIDING TRANSPORT lines — consultation had management with Brigade Major of 146ᵗʰ BRIGADE for disinfecting the blankets of the various battalions of the Brigade. THRESH DISINFECTOR working again.	W.W.A.

WAR DIARY
or
INTELLIGENCE SUMMARY

Army Form C. 2118.

Hour, Date, Place	Summary of Events and Information	Remarks and references to Appendices
June 24th WORMHOUDT	Visited 3rd BATTERY RFA BLICK. When the known they had expect until moved fill by similar authentic information moved in 3 days to 15th BDE RFA HQ. of the Ridge of ZAGGERS Visit to Quinquisto School anxious not the Ridge of ZAGGERS — CAPPEL to have it supplied ottomon blue fresh satisfactor. Noticed unquantity in ESQUELBEC, went and flood moving in at Convoy along to and to ZAGGERS — CAPPEL. Go to no Convoy v. [illegible] while heavy through the town, wthy further on yet. Visited 57th FIELD. Co. RE — who needed 3 horses — as I should have to take water for drinking from another — no trough has water for another from another pro — 3spps was taking horse Question in very pop — 3spps was taking horse Returns + minor shift trouble only. FODEN LORRY left from HERZEELE to distrib. rushes the 146th BDE + 9/12 W.R FLD AMBULANCE together with the Army SIGNAL SCHOOL. — to 148th BDE P/6 Gol retry willish the order [illegible] remainder 6	W/A

WAR DIARY
or
INTELLIGENCE SUMMARY

(Erase heading not required.)

Army Form C. 2118.

Hour, Date, Place	Summary of Events and Information	Remarks and references to Appendices
Jan 25th WORMHOUDT	Visited RIGHT SECTION & CENTRE of 2nd BDE. AMM. COL. who had excellent arrangement for transportation. Have great attention paid the as regards the horse & mules (which is all liked before being fed to them(?))	W.S.A.
Jan 26th WORMHOUDT	Inspected the SIGNAL CO. billets at ESQUELBEC – sanitary conditions moderate.	W.S.A.
Jan 27th WORMHOUDT	Inspected billets of 5th BATTERY & saw left Section of 2nd BDE. AMM. COL. – latter gone on as transportation (----) hd – to battery HP org regard good.	W.S.A.
Jan 28th WORMHOUDT	Work as usual.	W.S.A.
Jan 29th WORMHOUDT	Went to POPERINGHE – frozen about some stores left there	W.S.A.
Jan 30th WORMHOUDT	Inspected Ruthern hosp on outskirts of WORMHOUDT & and that forum has been made – reserving it away – (---- all more information to leaving & the ----)	W.S.A.

Army Form C. 2118.

WAR DIARY
or
INTELLIGENCE SUMMARY
(Erase heading not required.)

Instructions regarding War Diaries and Intelligence Summaries are contained in F. S. Regs., Part II. and the Staff Manual respectively. Title pages will be prepared in manuscript.

Hour, Date, Place	Summary of Events and Information	Remarks and references to Appendices
Jan 31st WORMHOUDT	Braising to marsh. Int FODEN LORRY to WINNEZEELE to do. 2 Companies R.E. & also A.S.C. SUPPLY COL.	W.S.R.

49th (W Riding) Sanit Section

Feb 1916
Mar

1/1 WR.
49 Div Sanitary
Sec

Feb

Vol 9

Army Form C. 2118.

WAR DIARY
or
INTELLIGENCE SUMMARY

(Erase heading not required.)

49th DIVISIONAL (WEST RIDING) SAN. SECTION

Hour, Date, Place	Summary of Events and Information	Remarks and references to Appendices
Feb. 1st WORMHOUDT	Work as usual. Reported damage done by cart of a kitchen coming for food to gate of my billet.	WNA
Feb. 2nd WORMHOUDT	Drew 2 days rations. Off FODEN LORRY BACK. Picking up & cleaning billet. Sanity work as usual.	WNA
Feb. 3rd WORMHOUDT	Handed over to San. Officer of 20th DIVISION. Since we entrained. Left billet about 6 pm. for CASSEL LORRY to come on but arrived by road. FODEN LORRY sent back to 14th DIVISION.	WNA
Feb. 4th TRAVELLING	In train until 1.45 pm when we detrained station at 3.30 — marched on near billet at PICQUIGNY. Left Sheet 17 Ⓑ ① . at 6.30 pm	WNA
Feb. 5th PICQUIGNY.	Met D.A.D.M.S. 7th DIVISION (New Interview) in afternoon. (Sheet 17 Ⓐ ①)	WNA
Feb. 6th PICQUIGNY.	Personal inspection of 7 DIV TRAIN at SOUES (Sheet 17 Ⓐ ①). Otherwise normal. 7 YORKSHIRE HUSSARS.	WNA
Feb. 7th PICQUIGNY.	Personal inspection of CABLE SECTION 6th CORPS. R.E. + DIV. SIGNAL Co. — other with two billets	WNA

Army Form C. 2118.

WAR DIARY
or
INTELLIGENCE SUMMARY
(Erase heading not required.)

Instructions regarding War Diaries and Intelligence Summaries are contained in F. S. Regs., Part II. and the Staff Manual respectively. Title pages will be prepared in manuscript.

Hour, Date, Place	Summary of Events and Information	Remarks and references to Appendices
Feb. 8. PICQUIGNY.	Work as usual. A letter of old friends' anniversaries, etc. Manoeuvres left by the President. Division moved on in the evening. Here we have in the evening. 7 WEST YORK. Billet also here. Journal visited H.Q. R.F.A. + 57th FIELD CO. R.E. thanks lines of transport arrangements	
Feb. 9. PICQUIGNY.		
Feb. 10. PICQUIGNY	Quarter master of 4' BDE AMM. COL. T'n BATTERY. the DIV. SUPPLY COL. Unharnessed	
Feb. 11. PICQUIGNY	Personal inspection of 3 BDE AMM. COL. + 6' BATTERY.	
Feb. 12. PICQUIGNY.	heart on to WARLOY: BAILLON. free reconnoitred. Motor Caravanned.	
Feb. 13. PICQUIGNY	Moved north section to WARLOY - BAILLON	
Feb. 14. WARLOY.	Started motor billet in WARLOY + had a billet at G. CORPS H.Q. Things not C. formed	
Feb. 15. WARLOY	Further inspection of WARLOY. Those nights to Town Major, inspected baths & the on. Slight alteration in heating arrangements.	

Army Form C. 2118.

WAR DIARY
or
INTELLIGENCE SUMMARY

(Erase heading not required.)

Instructions regarding War Diaries and Intelligence Summaries are contained in F.S. Regs., Part II. and the Staff Manual respectively. Title pages will be prepared in manuscript.

Hour, Date, Place	Summary of Events and Information	Remarks and references to Appendices
Feb. 16th WARLOY.	Visited SENLIS throughout the village & also arrange various parade matters with ADMS.	WNH
Feb. 17th WARLOY. Feb. 18 WARLOY.	Spent day at BOUZINCOURT going round billets & from — Spent day at BOUZINCOURT going round billets & from —	WNH
Feb 19th WARLOY	Visited HEDAUVILLE — to see if suitable Castles which was my Bgd. billet inspection at BOUZINCOURT still proving	WNH
Feb 20 WARLOY.	visited BAVELINCOURT to see how there were TYPHOID FEVER has been found among civilians in Latrine (a simple pit) could be constructed how to keep relative. Billets places been sprayed out with found sharp before.	WNH
Feb 21 WARLOY	Visited SENLIS transport & village with TOWN MAYOR to arrange about getting materials for incinerators.	WNH
Feb 22 WARLOY	Visited MARTINSART to inspect billets. Saw there one or two cases latter Typhy & one common urinal in the village. Rutter duty with town.	WNH
Feb 23 WARLOY	Visited ADMS at SENLIS to discuss sanitary measures billet inspection etc from various arsenal.	WNH

WAR DIARY or INTELLIGENCE SUMMARY

Army Form C. 2118.

Hour, Date, Place	Summary of Events and Information	Remarks and references to Appendices
Feb 24th WARLOY	Frosty. Spent day testing transit pumps to carry out with improvised Sanitary unit. Billet inspection round.	WNA
Feb 25th WARLOY	FODEN LORRY with THRESH DISINFECTORS arrived. The fridge burnt with the fuel so two discovered one broken. With the half the rate. Visited BOUZINCOURT & inspected a few billets there, also visited SENLIS & inspected some billets – were also snowing heavily. The rain as usual.	WNA
Feb 26 WARLOY	Snow hindered any efforts. Billet inspected. Disinfected a number of billets. Covered up.	WNA
Feb 27 WARLOY	Snow still hinders work. These arrangements slow. God respond for disinfector.	WNA
Feb 28 WARLOY	Visited AUTHUILLE. Inspected latrines & billets there of 5th WEST YORKSHIRE REGT + 5th BATTALION / K.O.Y.L.I. visited a number of billets with M.O. i/c Sanitary duties of WARLOY. Some work with THRESH D(ISINFECTOR	WNA
Feb 29 WARLOY	Same work with THRESH DISINFECTOR was repaired today.	WNA

49

Secretarys Section
Vol X

WAR DIARY
or
INTELLIGENCE SUMMARY

Army Form C. 2118.

4a ¹ W.R. Div. San. Section.

(Erase heading not required.)

Instructions regarding War Diaries and Intelligence Summaries are contained in F.S. Regs., Part II. and the Staff Manual respectively. Title pages will be prepared in manuscript.

Hour, Date, Place	Summary of Events and Information	Remarks and references to Appendices
March 1st WARLOY	Work as usual, billet inspection, & disinfection of blankets etc.	W.N.A.
March 2nd WARLOY	Work as usual, billet inspection.	W.N.A.
March 3rd WARLOY	Went to RUBEMPRÉ to look at billets, arranged about pulling up billets inspection rosters – weeks at ___ ___	W.N.A.
March 4th WARLOY – RUBEMPRÉ	Moved to RUBEMPRÉ – billets not very good – cleaned them up fairly well.	W.N.A.
March 5th RUBEMPRÉ	Proceeded with cleansing of billets, ensuring of water supply etc.	W.N.A.
March 6th RUBEMPRÉ	Moved & new billets in the village when there was a good supply of FODEN LORRY + THRESH for the disinfection of the clothing + room for the Sanitary DISINFECTOR	W.N.A.
March 7th RUBEMPRÉ	Maj. Sanitation inspection of village.	W.N.A.
March 8th RUBEMPRÉ	Visited Div. Cyclists at PUCHEVILLERS. Billet inspection at.	W.N.A.

WAR DIARY
or
INTELLIGENCE SUMMARY

(Erase heading not required.)

Army Form C. 2118.

Hour, Date, Place	Summary of Events and Information	Remarks and references to Appendices
March 9 RUBEMPRE	Consulted with Town Major about sanitation of village. Drew up report on FIRE PRECAUTIONS in billets.	WA
March 10 RUBEMPRE	Examined water supply of RUBEMPRE in an area taken up partly occupied by the FRENCH was not finished.	WA
March 11 RUBEMPRE	Visited 1/5 KOYLI + RMA at PUCHEVILLERS. The sanitary condition of the RMA. was very bad - rutted all over + latrines in bad position etc. Work as usual.	WA
March 12 RUBEMPRE	FODEN with THRESH working steadily.	WA
March 13 RUBEMPRE	Visited ADMS - with other O.C.'s of FLD. AMBULANCES at conference. Other work as usual.	WA
March 14 RUBEMPRE	Visited 2/5 W.YORK REGT + 1/8 W.YORK. REGT. at Varennes - first one sanitary arrangements & billets on the whole good, but not much apps.	WA

WAR DIARY or INTELLIGENCE SUMMARY

Army Form C. 2118.

Hour, Date, Place	Summary of Events and Information	Remarks and references to Appendices
March 15th RUBEMPRE	Visited 5 W. YORK REGT at HARPONVILLE — notified M.O. all cleaned up found all men billets. Return to HQ v. Poor. 7 W. YORK REGT No pmt up & has own billet spetus. Saw TOWN MAJOR of VARENNES regard dry canvas hutts by April 19. I chef. Ill manner kept in billets. This where is O.C. to even for. (weather fine) - Drew apponent for L/Cpl JERRISON L/Cpl for BASE.	W.T.H.
MARCH 16 RUBEMPRE	Arranged to get 10 labor men to help in FODEN LORRY not THRESH. Started weekly Disinfector by Night as well as day. 1st FLD. AMBULANCE	W.T.H.
March 17th RUBEMPRE	Visited LOUVENCOURT — saw the billets, canteen and tour the place is being cleaned up	W.T.H.
March 18th RUBEMPRE " 19th " " 20 "	Work as usual.	W.T.H.

WAR DIARY or INTELLIGENCE SUMMARY

Army Form C. 2118.

Hour, Date, Place	Summary of Events and Information	Remarks and references to Appendices
March 21st RUBEMPRÉ	Visited CANDAS & inspected Baths. There was but no up for sufficient number of men. Arranged with the proof & matron. Then changed 6th & 8th YORK & LANC REGT. I ordered as to treaty the men, also visited PIERREGOT — which was in a comfortable clean condition.	WSF
March 22nd RUBEMPRÉ	Visited BEAUCOURT — fairly clean & sanitary, men disinfected. Visited BEHENCOURT and disinfected SCABIES Billets — otherwise as usual.	WSF
March 23rd RUBEMPRÉ	Visited CONTAY — difficulty in keeping all the place clean as the FRENCH occupy part of the village. Visited MOLLIENS au BOIS — said was pretty clean. Visited LOUVENCOURT — saw TOWN MAJOR about k-ponds which have never had small — nothing can be done except put crude oil on surface & prevent mosquito breeding there. Town otherwise in good sanitary condition & it were being defined to parents.	WSF
March 24th RUBEMPRÉ	Visited CONTAY — BEHENCOURT — fullworks — had men good — clean billets & village kept clean — visited SENLIS & found billets were improving from a sanitary point of view.	WSF

WAR DIARY
or
INTELLIGENCE SUMMARY

(Erase heading not required.)

Army Form C. 2118.

Hour, Date, Place	Summary of Events and Information	Remarks and references to Appendices
Wed 25 RUBEMPRÉ	Work as usual	W/R
" 26 "	Work as usual. Burning most of day to clear up as much work. Work with FODEN LORRY & THRESH DISINFECTOR carried on as usual	W/R
" 27 "	Visited HARPONVILLE Rev — DIPHTHERIA case among the civilians has ceased. Arranged for disinfection of billet on next day, village quite clean & put on machine — worker	W/R
" 28 RUBEMPRÉ	Rain wds ruined billet.	W/R
" 29 " RUBEMPRÉ	Rain as usual	W/R
" 30 " RUBEMPRE	Visited CANAPLES & SEPTENVILLE to machine Gun Co. 4th BDE. otherwise as usual. REINFORCEMENT from BASE.	W/R
" 31 " RUBEMPRÉ	Visited LA VICOGNE + two 1/7 W.R. REGT still studying blankets for scissors etc. as usual.	W/R

WAR DIARY

of 49th (W.R.) Divisional Sanitary Section

for the month of April 1916

COMMITTEE FOR THE
MEDICAL HISTORY OF THE WAR

Date   9- JUN. 1916

49

Sanitary Sect.

Vol XI

WAR DIARY

INTELLIGENCE SUMMARY 49th (WR) Divisional Sanitary Section

Army Form C. 2118.

(Erase heading not required.)

Instructions regarding War Diaries and Intelligence Summaries are contained in F. S. Regs., Part II. and the Staff Manual respectively. Title pages will be prepared in manuscript.

Hour, Date, Place	Summary of Events and Information	Remarks and references to Appendices
April 1st 1916 RUBEMPRÉ	Work as usual. Billets of troops were trimmed & were in satisfactory condition. Disinfection of blankets.	W.R.A.
April 2nd 1916 RUBEMPRÉ	Visited NAOURS to see new billet for Sanitary Section. Church work as usual.	W.R.A.
April 3rd 1916 RUBEMPRÉ	—	W.R.A.
April 4th 1916 RUBEMPRÉ	Moved to NAOURS in afternoon leaving a small party behind to clean up billet etc.	W.R.A.
April 5th 1916 NAOURS	Finished the move — billet at RUBEMPRÉ left clean & W R Division approved. Proceeded through village completing visit MOEUVRES en BOIS in satisfactory condition by no division. Was left in satisfactory condition by no division. Stamp blankets serving as usual billets. Work as usual.	W.R.A.
April 6th 1916 NAOURS	The FODEN LORRY & THRESH DISINFECTORS had been found on the road-side — on starting the road in any way, but instructing the matter of running it, no oil, no file could be used, both for further information without taking out disinfield articles. This lorry up infect articles. Taking out disinfield articles. This lorry up started operations. Temperature of 220° F what is required to kill lice etc. TENT & presence of 60 lb. on the pressure gauge & the temperature was necessary. The safety valve has therefore to be screwed down till the line assured for 1 & the values are then kept & the pressure. Then was found & the effective to kill lice etc, if not more. 10 Blankets could get in each cage i.e. 20 in each cylinder. This number is reduced by 33⅓% on the	W.R.A.

WAR DIARY

INTELLIGENCE SUMMARY

Army Form C. 2118.

(Erase heading not required.)

Instructions regarding War Diaries and Intelligence Summaries are contained in F. S. Regs., Part II. and the Staff Manual respectively. Title pages will be prepared in manuscript.

Hour, Date, Place	Summary of Events and Information	Remarks and references to Appendices
April 7th NAOURS.	No enemy aircraft was over today. 30 in rank today. 30 blankets and boots has been taken from Laundry in the middle of the night in the cages. Visited LA VICOGNE. Here the 7. W.R. REGT. were formed. The village was clean. Spare accommodation for advance accommodation of reinforce men in 2 serjeants huts. There was no road.	W.A.A.
April 8th NAOURS.	Visited various units in NAOURS — 4th W.R. Regt. HQrs. 5th W.R. Regt. / finds satisfactory Bde Cyclist Co. Div Sch.	W.A.A.
April 9th NAOURS.	Also visited TALMAS when I came to 148th BDE MACHINE GUN CO. It has made a great improvement in their billet since they came in. Visited BATHS which will be opened in a few days & hot-water arrangement. Provided showers with soap-trays at hand there at one. Visited WARGNIES 2d W.R. Field Amb. & ½ Co. R.E. Billets pretty clean. Billets inspection wasting of Pendukieu road.	W.A.A.
April 10th NAOURS.	Attended conference at A.D.M.S: Office in morning & a medical board in afternoon. Saw 5 WEST YORK. REGT. Billets at VIGNACOURT — afternoon.	W.A.A.

Army Form C. 2118.

WAR DIARY
of
INTELLIGENCE SUMMARY
(Erase heading not required.)

Instructions regarding War Diaries and Intelligence Summaries are contained in F. S. Regs., Part II. and the Staff Manual respectively. Title pages will be prepared in manuscript.

Hour, Date, Place	Summary of Events and Information	Remarks and references to Appendices
April 11th NAOURS	Work as usual. Built incinerator & have divided clothing from the Divisional Clothing Dump. Raind.	GWA
" 12th NAOURS	Visited TALMAS but could not find TOWN MAJOR & what I saw was no trade otherwise as usual.	GWA
" 13th NAOURS	Visited HALLOY WARGNIES when two Frenchmen were interpreters — no Scabies 1129 patients, they flock to them. Both had very fair arrangements for removing dung from the rivulet which was working well. Also visited PERNOIS and BERTRANCOURT. Every Town Mayor is being advised to do his utmost MAYORS of the Towns to do all manure shall be removed by civilians if possible if not with the help of the military authorities by a certain specified date. 2 weeks is about the average time given to do it in.	
	Great difficulty to persuade in getting carry [...] chlorine solution fresden & troops trips etc. so that the work can only be done very gradually will report in them things.	WWA
" 14th NAOURS	Visited TALMAS and BATHS which were not quite satisfactory, but want to make sure that has been got, & the troops was being made.	
" 15th "		
" 16th NAOURS.	Visited VIGNACOURT — TOWN 146th BDE MACHINE GUN Co. and A.S.C. 466 Co. with ambulets of the 8 WEST YORKSHIRE REGT. The BDE MACHINE GUN CO. has some bad billets their sanitary arrangement was poor. They handed over [...] on the 17th	GWA

1247 W 3299 200,000 (E) 8/14 J.B.C. & A. Forms/C. 2118/11.

WAR DIARY
or
INTELLIGENCE SUMMARY
(Erase heading not required.)

Army Form C. 2118.

Hour, Date, Place	Summary of Events and Information	Remarks and references to Appendices
April 17 NAOURS	Work as usual.	WNH
" 18 NAOURS	Visited TALMAS and saw 3rd MOBILE REPAIR UNIT (4th ARMY), the 6th ARMY BUS COMPANY & Sand billets of the 4th K.O.Y.L.I. also saw the 2nd attatched. Also the Army Corps haven't put in position, had it was not satisfactory yet & needs more tiffle plates securing in it.	WNH
" 19 " 20 NAOURS	Visited VIGNACOURT. — Here I inspected billets of 1st/6th W.YORK REGT + 8th W.YORK and the 146th BDE. M.G. Co. — The Callen of Vigneau has all been much improved. The garrison major was also interviewed & spent with him to the Mayor's town	WNH
" 21 NAOURS	Visited LA VICOGNE. Found the 7th W RIDING REGT. — here the East tetgroom it Satisfactory & the Town major was informed. The M.O. was interviewed about the troop baths at the aftelium Renclen. also saw M.G. Co. of 148th BDE where sanitary arrangement needs attention.	WNH
" 28 NAOURS	General Disinfection:— refer working at full pressure — Am trying to flood with Cresol fort, stored in the Dugouts in Naours & then the Cliff & the houses and in return for infected blankets.	WNH

Army Form C. 2118.

WAR DIARY
or
INTELLIGENCE SUMMARY
(Erase heading not required.)

Hour, Date, Place	Summary of Events and Information	Remarks and references to Appendices
April 22nd NAOURS (continued)	The Reptrs. and Lewis Gunners put when the flank is not required by this now.	W.R.A.
April 23rd NAOURS	Visited 5th WEST RIDING REGT LEWIS GUNNERS and 147th MACHINE GUN CO. at NAOURS and 3rd MOBILE REPAIR UNIT, 148th BDE MACHINE GUN CO: the Bus Co: at TALMAS. That went on road.	L.R.A.
24 NAOURS	Visited HALLOY — saw a large no. of fullde in the village. at Conference of ADMS. Other present B.C's & Division.	W.R.A.
25 NAOURS	Wrote no travel	
26 NAOURS	Visited VADENCOURT — saw BATHS & LAUNDRY NOTTON M.O i/c. About filled here re. disinfector bldg. & A.S.C. in NAOURS and 1/2 W.R. Fld. Amb. & VAL DE MAISON. This work newel.	E.R.A.
27 NAOURS	Visited. CANAPLES — saw — on 4th BDE. (HOW) R.F.A. Held. also DIV. SIGNALLERS at NAOURS. New work in Disinfector and sprayer at Dullut with Pannier & available in assent just now. Casn, & a GERMAN MEASLES outbreak.	B.D.A. L.R.A.

1247 W 3299 200,000 (E) 8/14 J.B.C. & A. Forms/C. 2118/11.

WAR DIARY
or
INTELLIGENCE SUMMARY

(Erase heading not required.)

Army Form C. 2118.

Hour, Date, Place	Summary of Events and Information	Remarks and references to Appendices
April 28. NAOURS	Conference with ADMS, O.C.'s of Ambulances 2/1 York. Hussars. Visited billets of YORK. HUSSARS at NAOURS. CANAPLES & Julien. Mobile Vet. Section not much infected sent to most of the men being away for work. FODEN LORRY with THRESH DISINFECTOR.	W.N.T
April 29. NAOURS	Visited billets of A.S.C. to NAOURS. AMMN COL. other ranks in and MACHINE GUN Co. of 14th Bde.	W.N.T
April 30. NAOURS.	FODEN Lorry cleaned. Arranged with ARTILLERY SCHOOL at HAVERNAS to send the Foden Lorry with Thresh Disinfector over to them for 2 days.	W.N.T

4th Div. Sanit. Section

May 1916

Army Form C. 2118.

Med

WAR DIARY
or
INTELLIGENCE SUMMARY   49th (W.R.) Division Sanitary Section
(Erase heading not required.)

Instructions regarding War Diaries and Intelligence Summaries are contained in F. S. Regs., Part II. and the Staff Manual respectively. Title pages will be prepared in manuscript.

Hour, Date, Place	Summary of Events and Information	Remarks and references to Appendices
MAY 1st NAOURS.	Conference with A.D.M.S. Other work as usual.	W.N.A.
May 2nd NAOURS	Visited 4" Bde R.F.A. at CANAPLES + Div. Amm. Col. at PERNOIS. Arranged for supervision of sanitary arrangements of same.	W.N.A.
May 3rd NAOURS.	Went out billet 6 W.R. Regt at NAOURS. Reps hyppus being made in deulu, emptied .... Other work as usual.	W.N.A.
May 4th NAOURS.	Visited VIGNACOURT + saw 6 W.Y. billets - some ypds? Much work tas probs of stagnant water & mango..... ...... Visited 146" Bde M.G. Co. showing staff ..... also saw 1 W.R. Field Amb. - re-examined their .... mosquito breeding	W.N.A.
May 5th NAOURS.	Visited TALMAS - saw 5 York + Lanc Regt, 146" Bde + Trench Mortar Battery - all with satisfactory sanitary arrangements. Arranged to have certain ponds .... stagnant pools & ...... with creosote to prevent mosquito breeding	W.N.A.
May 6th NAOURS.	Visited various billets in NAOURS. Other work as usual. YORKSHIRE HUSSARS left NAOURS - billets left fairly clean.	W.N.A.
May 7th NAOURS	Wrote up weekly report to A.D.M.S. Saw A.D.V.S. about arrangements for hiring stores for Packets + ... arrangements for billet at NAOURS - Div School, Military Police etc	W.N.A.

WAR DIARY
or
INTELLIGENCE SUMMARY
(Erase heading not required.)

Army Form C. 2118.

Hour, Date, Place	Summary of Events and Information	Remarks and references to Appendices
May 8th 1916. NAOURS.	Work as usual. Dissatisfied with billets - flea bit - sprayed disinfectant with it! K RLL hospital closed. 500 blankets taken over to VAL DE MAISON for storage. Papers in order then presented by Field Ambulance.	O.C. Saw Leslie on leave to England.
" 9th 1916. NAOURS	Work as usual. Raining.	
" 10th 1916. NAOURS.	Work as usual.	WA
" 11th 1916. NAOURS.	Work as usual. Another 500 blankets taken to VAL DE MAISON. Burnt old clothing from Divisional DUMP. Otherwise no news.	
" 12th 1916. NAOURS.	Work as before. Raining all day.	
" 13th 1916. NAOURS.	Work as usual.	
" 14th 1916. NAOURS.		
" 15th		
" 16th		
" 17th 1916. NAOURS.	Minor troubles among men in hosp. visits 140 BDE. MACHINE GUN. Co. - stopped sanitary arrangements	WA
" 18th 1916. "	Visited NORTH IRISH HORSE (C. Squad) at VAL DE MAISON - their complaint was unfortified water - have only moved into the billet for 3 days. Visited DUMP where khaki was given.	WA

Army Form C. 2118.

WAR DIARY
or
INTELLIGENCE SUMMARY

(Erase heading not required.)

Instructions regarding War Diaries and Intelligence Summaries are contained in F. S. Regs., Part II. and the Staff Manual respectively. Title pages will be prepared in manuscript.

Hour, Date, Place		Summary of Events and Information	Remarks and references to Appendices
May. 20 1916	NAOURS	Visited Machine Gun Co. A.S.C. Co. & Trench Mortar Batt. of 146¹ Bde. ranges practise alterations to be carried out. also visited 464 C. A.S.C. at NAOURS & the Divisional School. Otherwise as usual.	Init.
May. 21 1916.	NAOURS.	Visited W. ARQUEVES. Otherwise as usual.	W.N.A.
May. 22 1916.	NAOURS	Visited VIGNACOURT. Inspected billets of 8 West York. Regt. advised that should allow be removed from all billets where straw pallet, & where there was no such straw, to remove the men into bivouacs. This was to get rid of lice. Otherwise as usual.	W.N.A.
May. 23 1916.	NAOURS.	Visited BERTAUCOURT. Saw billets of _ Bde. R.F.A. Some alterations & improvements in sanitary commenced. Otherwise as usual.	W.N.A.
May. 24 1916	NAOURS.	Visited VIGNACOURT — Saw billets of 6" West York. Regt. — faulty drain near _ afternoon. Otherwise as usual. Honeysuckle _	W.N.A.
May 25 1916 26.	NAOURS.	_ as usual. Speared Rest, passed it.	W.N.A.

WAR DIARY
or
INTELLIGENCE SUMMARY

(Erase heading not required.)

Army Form C. 2118.

Instructions regarding War Diaries and Intelligence Summaries are contained in F. S. Regs., Part II. and the Staff Manual respectively. Title pages will be prepared in manuscript.

Hour, Date, Place	Summary of Events and Information	Remarks and references to Appendices
MAY 27th 1916 NAOURS	Visited CANAPLES to see about Brecken round with M.O. i/c BATHS re BATH HOUSE had before ordering them etc. suggested builder of elastic staples which improves ventilation etc. accompanying billets Asso. Co. here on proposed various alterations to facility arrangements also gas gas lectures billets. at NAOURS	W.N.A
May 28th 1916 NAOURS	Visited TALMAS & saw billets of MACHINE GUN Co. & TRENCH MORTAR Co. The work as usual.	W.N.A
MAY 29th 1916 NAOURS	Visited AMIENS with A.D.M.S. trying a brand to be used to Cavy every comfort & fuel in towns after their journey out.	W.N.A
MAY 30th 1916 NAOURS	Left & rode down a new route with A.D.M.S. Visited VIGNACOURT – lately had an Ambulance billet; HALLOY where some billets have now which has been sick of preserved cripples. They been seen the time's PERNOIS Vicity D.A.C. billets cleaned & all have billets with field past. Also at BERTAUCOURT – the place had been this billets now found. a large part of the ARTILLERY units there cleaned up considerable & saw their billets in description Cavalier has left. Learnt about	W.N.A
MAY 31st 1916 NAOURS	Went round to billets at TALMAS – many things have left the village to their billets, was left built down in the MG. Latrines etc. to billets and found brought to a very satisfactory state. BATHS there are very good & have every gear that pollution apparatus which looks excellently. A new brown of Shelley from soap trap.	W.N.A

1247 W 3299 200,000 (E) 8/14 J.B.C. & A. Forms/C. 2118/11.

49th Div. Sanitation

June 1915.

COMMITTEE FOR THE
MEDICAL HISTORY OF THE WAR
Date 31 AUG. 1915

WAR DIARY
or
INTELLIGENCE SUMMARY 49th (W.R.) Div. Sanitary Section

Army Form C. 2118

(Erase heading not required.)

Place	Date	Hour	Summary of Events and Information	Remarks and references to Appendices
NAOURS	1 June 1916	—	Visited TALMAS with DADMS. LoFaire & DADMS (Sanitation) 4th ARMY — went Reference to LtCol Smyth. The pump devised not to be used for drinking water, but another pump to be put in use meant for drinking water.	
"	2 Jun	"	Visited VADENCOURT — Sewn Baths. Then showed visited one unit in NAOURS with	
"	3 "	"	Went with ADMS to AMIENS. Tried to find & pump sewage into the Canal. Came away from billet & jumped in to the Canal. ASC company, Baths, — 248th BSe RFA obviated the unit & CHIPILLY — Enquired about allocation & form of sanitary arrangements. Visited R.E. R.G. at TALMAS.	
"	4 "	"	Captain at ADMS' office — visited. Fair Hospital & R.E. about providing to attend & carry the camel about fluid roll in and with the VDANGE PUMP.	
"	5 "	"	FODEN LORRY with THRESH DISINFECTORS has been away for last 2 days being repaired. Came back in afternoon.	
"	6 "	"	Visited CANAPLES with DADMS & the BATHS &c.	
"	7 "	"	Visited VAL DE MAISON (The Officers running new arrangements put up by L 3rd W.R. Field Ambulance	co-A.A
"	8 "	"	During this heat 8 days some stoneworkers have been gone — but as 1) Spraying huts &c to prevent mosquito breed up in the 2) Disinfect blankets in Thresh. Infects (in other carts) 3) Disinfecting various billets for infected houses 4) Other minor improvements in sanitary matters & different units.	

Army Form C. 2118.

WAR DIARY
or
INTELLIGENCE SUMMARY
(Erase heading not required.)

Instructions regarding War Diaries and Intelligence Summaries are contained in F.S. Regs., Part II. and the Staff Manual respectively. Title Pages will be prepared in manuscript.

Places	Date	Hour	Summary of Events and Information	Remarks and references to Appendices
NAOURS	9th June 1916		Visited Troops – Trent now billets at 4 K.O.Y.L.I. Regt, 148th Bde Machine G. Co., A.S.C. 18th Bde Co. – also the Batts. – No. 3 Mobile Repair Unit. Work normal.	W.H.
	10th		Visited WARLOY, PUCHVILLERS (See Advanced Med. Dept.?), VADENCOURT (See Batts), with A.D.M.S.	W.H.
	11th		Visited Billets at NAOURS. Work normal.	
	12th 13th 14th 15th		Packing up units & move to fresh place. Visited Val de Maison billets & camp about noon, then the next day.	W.H.
NAOURS to VAL DE MAISON	16th		Moved Section to VAL DE MAISON (M.36.a.8-4. Sheet 57D). All men put into Bivouacs.	
VAL DE MAISON	17th		Visited RUBEMPRÉ – PIERREGOT with Asst Sanitary arrangement. Before leaving NAOURS, 1800 Blankets were distributed from the Division & handed to Ordnance. The issue of the Divisional area was handed by the Division and left in very clean condition.	W.H.

WAR DIARY
or
INTELLIGENCE SUMMARY

Army Form C. 2118

Place	Date	Hour	Summary of Events and Information	Remarks and references to Appendices
VAL DE MAISON	15th June 1916		Visited SEPTENVILLE & from 1st W.R. Fld. Amb. — The Men Stan Taken over was in a very clean condition.	
"	19th		Conference at A.D.M.S's Office in Toutencourt.	
"	20th		Visited ACHVILLERS, G.W.Y. in camp, all tents inspected got into new toplets, funded for addition trench. Stoval reconnade by R.E.s. Visited MIRVAUX — saw billets of D.A.C. & 248 Bde. R.F.A. tents pns, tents erected doing their burnes for billets, arrival in front.	
"	21st		Visited 146th Bde. H.Q. at HERISSART — and 148 Bde. M.G. Co. at TOUTENCOURT	
"	22nd		Work as usual	
"	23rd		Visited TOUTENCOURT — saw 148th Bde. H.Q. & Camp of 4th & 5th Y&L. Regt. The latrines were rather griffey and they seem to run the hut.	
"	24th 25th		Work as usual.	
"	26th		SANITARY Section moved to RUBEMPRE. Two men left at Corps Dump to guard it, and the FODEN LORRY with TORESH DISINFECTOR was also left with gitroups & two men took it for the benefit of the 3rd W.R. Field Ambulance. Visited POREEVILLE & lote for a place to move the Corps Dump to & from 2LtRich ADMS.	

Army Form C. 2118

WAR DIARY
or
INTELLIGENCE SUMMARY
(*Erase heading not required.*)

Instructions regarding War Diaries and Intelligence Summaries are contained in F.S. Regs., Part II. and the Staff Manual respectively. Title Pages will be prepared in manuscript.

Place	Date	Hour	Summary of Events and Information	Remarks and references to Appendices
RUBEMPRE	27th June		Put all Sanitary manifolds of SAN. SECTION to HOSPITAL saturated by the Section of the 3rd W.R. Field Amb. in order. Rainy weather.	W/A
"	28th		Both no rained all week work hard so all units are moving about preparatory to an advance. Rainy weather.	W/A
"	29th		Kilwinkler + Scott went for new Motor Lorry returned from Both. Rainy.	W/A
"	30th		Began to remove medical stores it to far VAL DE MAISON DUMP to FORCEVILLE Chapelle heather.	W/A

1875 Wt. W593/826 1,000,000 4/15 J.B.C. & A. A.D.S.S./Forms/C. 2118.

49th (W.R.) Divl. Sany. Section

July 1916.

WAR DIARY or INTELLIGENCE SUMMARY

Army Form C. 2118

49th (W.R) Div. Sanitary Section

Vol 14

Place	Date	Hour	Summary of Events and Information	Remarks and references to Appendices
VAL DE MAISON	July 1st 1916		Remaining collecting residual stores to FORCEVILLE.	W.A.A
"	July 2		Moved permanently there with the Section, leaving 2 men in charge of remaining dumps.	W.A.A
FORCEVILLE	July 3 4 5		visited MARTINSART — and arranged for motor lorry to be at MARTINSART under Col. Whalley's orders. Had a fatigue party arranged for MARTINSART with 2 Sanitary Section CORPORALS in charge. Chosen by MARTINSART under the direction of the Town Major. 90 men with an officer appointed later on this purpose.	W.A.A
"	6 7 8		visited HEDAUVILLE — visited various billets & units there. Have seen a fatigue party for the village, and also to run to FORCEVILLE.	W.A.A
"	9 10 11		Have MARTINSART, HEDAUVILLE and FORCEVILLE cleaned up of their refuse passing through to cart to dump. A very large amount of rubbish has to be burnt & all the latrines has to be cleaned. Billets are pretty clean, latrines	W.A.A
"	12	—	MARTINSART now in a satisfactory condition. Rubbish disposed of. emptied	W.A.A
"	13	9	FORCEVILLE pretty satisfactory now. New troops coming through some stayed a few days — 4 YORKS. LANCASTER Regt. to came into the Camp here.	W.A.A
"	14			
"	15		LORRY has 2 newstaps put on. Other work is usual.	
"	16		REINFORCEMENTS for battalions in FORCEVILLE arranged. Have a fatigue party from them to keep their billets clean & their latrines in Sanitary situation.	W.A.A

WAR DIARY
or
INTELLIGENCE SUMMARY
(Erase heading not required.)

Army Form C. 2118

Place	Date	Hour	Summary of Events and Information	Remarks and references to Appendices
FORCEVILLE	July 17		at Sunday conference with DADMS & Reserve Army.	Wolff
"	18 / 19 / 20 / 21		5th month as usual. FODEN LORRY removed from RUBEMPRE to CLAIRFAYE. Went & stopped with 1/2 WR Fd. Ambulance. Putting Sanitary arrangements of camps at FORCEVILLE in good order. Cleaning up the village, more latrine accommodation being provided & fallen for proper arrangement. Two large sheds + shops are billeted temporarily in the village.	Wolff 6/1/.
"	22		Making Soap-trap for BATHS at VARENNES. Builders commenced at FORCEVILLE.	Wolff
"	23		Builder commenced at HEDAUVILLE & fully. Soap-trap in at BATHS. Sick cleaning up	Wolff
"	24 / 25		before 31st in villages of HEDAUVILLE, FORCEVILLE, VARENNES.	
"	26		Visited LANCASHIRE DUMP P.35.C.5.1. Sheet 57 D.S.E. + Co. DUMP across BLACKHORSE BRIDGE at W.5.d.7.2. Sheet 57 D.S.E. Where noxious Cup. accumulations of refuse have formed. These were reported on to 15 ADMS & means suggested of preventing it.	Wolff
"	27 / 28 / 29 / 30		Putting up DIVISIONAL INCINERATORS at HEDAUVILLE - 3 closed ones & two large closed ones for rubbish also. Where are town refuse suffered from at 2 Dumps mentioned above are faulty by either spread indiscriminate at FORCEVILLE to town rubbish. Bath Greg Kipp made at BATHS are very satisfactory. Allowed a MEDICAL BOARD at HEDAUVILLE on 30th.	Wolff
"	31		Stoke Sanita. refuse from LEALVILLERS & VARENNES & these are not of no over, being horses no mare at VARENNES. & these are kept high at BATHS.	Wolff

49th (W.R.) Divisional Sanitary Section

August 1916

Army Form C. 2118

WAR DIARY
or
INTELLIGENCE SUMMARY
(Erase heading not required.)

49th (W.R.) DIVISIONAL SANITARY SECTION

VC/15

Place	Date	Hour	Summary of Events and Information	Remarks and references to Appendices
FORCEVILLE	August 1st		Work as usual.	[initials]
"	2nd		Occasional visits to 25th Div. A.S.C. (Div. Train). Incinerator fields at HEDAUVILLE still working hard. Having rubbish from LANCASHIRE DUMP. Otherwise as usual.	[initials]
"	3rd		Visited WAGON LINES of all 49 A Div. ARTILLERY & AMMUNITION COLUMN, also of ARTILLERY & AMM. COL. left by 48th Div. The men consisted with the Woods Command & of HEDAUVILLE. 7th WEST YORKSHIRE REGT left their billets in FORCEVILLE — same of them being very dirty. These were reported to the A.D.M.S.	[initials]
"	4th 5th		work as usual. weather hot.	[initials]
"	6th		Visited MARTINSART — inspected billets there & civilian's last has left. There was an empty cellar rather full of latrines also not emptied. The cops in the cutting also leave there about the roads. A number of fatigue men. Village as fatigue parties are to get from any large men. I took 1 NCO & fatigue men with 2 NC.O.s sent to BLACK HORSE BRIDGE & path 1 foot wide running from the DUMP at SOUTH BLUFF & carry it to from the BLACKHORSE ROAD meets the HAMEL-ALBERT ROAD, where LORRIES could shove it to the DIVISIONAL Incinerators at HEDAUVILLE.	
"	7th		2 NCOs sent out to MARTINSART to see is charge of fatigue party there also are to clean up the village. & also BLACKHORSE BRIDGE post visited LANCASHIRE DUMP which is now cleaned, and the amount placed in SOUTH BLUFF — Rise in difference has been made in the Refuse being cleaned daily, but no amount being cleaned daily.	[initials]

WAR DIARY
or
INTELLIGENCE SUMMARY
(Erase heading not required.)

Army Form C. 2118

Place	Date	Hour	Summary of Events and Information	Remarks and references to Appendices
FORCEVILLE	Aug 8		Orders were given to prevent any further desecration of turf which at SOUTH BLUFF. Removal of rubbish from here to HAMEL – ALBERT road is being proceeded with. FORCEVILLE. The men are clean and sanitary conveniences are being kept in good order at Camp for Reinforcements etc.	WD/App
	9		Removed pickets from South Bluff by motor lorry to HEDAUVILLE. Took an inventory. Remaining pickets for South Bluff in positions there & every where ready for a move. Went on scheme for north & south.	WD/App
	10th 11th 12th 13th 14th 15th 16th 17th		As above. Still removing rubbish from South Bluff dump. A certain amount is being burned there is still litter also, otherwise as usual — inspecting billets etc.	WD/App
	18th		Rubbish for dump at South Bluff nearly all removed.	WD/App
	19th		Took over BATHS at ACHEUX from 25th Division in preparation for putting our Division into the back area west of the line.	
	20th 21st 22		Visit & moved into the back area. 146th & 147th Brigade at ACHEUX. Bathing men of 146th & 147th Brigade at ACHEUX. Division lines moved to. Sent out sanitary squads to reconnoitre villages where the Division has moved to.	WD/App

1875 Wt. W593/826 1,000,000 4/15 J.B.C. & A. A.D.S.S./Forms/C. 2118.

WAR DIARY
or
INTELLIGENCE SUMMARY
(Erase heading not required.)

Army Form C. 2118

Instructions regarding War Diaries and Intelligence Summaries are contained in F.S. Regs., Part II. and the Staff Manual respectively. Title Pages will be prepared in manuscript.

Place	Date	Hour	Summary of Events and Information	Remarks and references to Appendices
FORCEVILLE	August 23rd		visited billets in ARQUEVES & PUCHVILLERS	WWH
"	24		Went round billets at ACHEUX. Thurcock as usual. BATHS still running.	WWH
"	25		Visited ARQUEVES — arrangement made to visit also RAINCHEVAL. Chapman sanitary corporal called to advise as no provision for troops in any quantity has previously been made. Inspected a billet there & disinfection case has been arranged to spray the billets & utensils & billet effects.	WWH
"	26		Bathing as usual. Conference re A.D.M.S. in present	WWH
"	27		Took over BATHS at ACHEUX totally for 25th Division. On our Division is now moving into the line again.	WWH
"	28		Went round billets in FORCEVILLE & to visit the left the village — was left sick — chief was sent billet at HEDAUVILLE vacated by 25 D. — my duty & also visited billet at HEDAUVILLE vacated by 25th Div.	WWH
"	29		Went round billets in FORCEVILLE & to ADMS's & to ADMS's regarding the village. Rest of our Division left PUCHVILLERS which has considerably cleaner than when we entered it. RAINCHEVAL & ARQUEVES handed over vacated by French Division & the billets left clean FORCEVILLE branches was taken over again. Wet weather.	WWH
"	30		Very wet weather. At a conference on this J ADMS in afternoon It was arranged as usual no passes can be done cutting up the wealth work in the line.	WWH
"	31		Fine weather again. Nearly all troops in the line. Baths at ACHEUX still being run.	WWH

1875 Wt. W593/826 1,000,000 4/15 J.B.C. & A. A.D.S.S./Forms/C. 2118.

49th (W.R.) Divl. San. Sect.

Oct 1916

COMMITTEE FOR THE
MEDICAL HISTORY OF THE WAR

Date 26 OCT. 1916

WAR DIARY
or
INTELLIGENCE SUMMARY

Army Form C. 2118

(Erase heading not required.)

49th (W.R.) Divisional Sanitary Section

Vol 15

Place	Date	Hour	Summary of Events and Information	Remarks and references to Appendices
FORCEVILLE	Sept. 1. 2. 1916		Working with 1/2nd W.R. Fd. Ambulance and in orders of the C.O. of that unit, dragging wounded who were coming through the Ambulance in large numbers.	L/Cpl
"	3.		Ordinary work of Section being carried on as usual.	Cpl
"	4. 5.		Visited billets & Camp at FORCEVILLE, also visited HEDAUVILLE and incinerator patrol etc. Other work as usual.	L/Cpl
"	6. 7. 8. 9.		Work on billets at BATHS as usual. 146th & 147th Brigades came out of trenches and had left Brigades bathed. Both HEDAUVILLE & FORCEVILLE being put into very clean sanitary condition. On last day the villages were shelled. The 2nd Fuel Ambulance left the villages as they burnt stables away the hospital billets say S. Div. Train. (A.S.C.) also, knows their billets were burnt into up the village.	L/Cpl
"	10. 11. 12. 13.		Cleaning up manure horse lines & throw places in FORCEVILLE. Pre shelled & many returned. Other work as usual. Men billets in FORCEVILLE that have vacated by fatigue party.	L/Cpl
"	14. 15. 16.		Visited transport lines of 148th Brigade in FORCEVILLE. 146th Brigade Transport lines which has been vacated & left dirty & has vacated it up. A.P.T. talk for the units responsible who cleaned it up.	L/Cpl
"	17. 18. 19. 20. 21. 22. 23. 24.		Had A.minister Field at HEDAUVILLE cleaned up as it was getting too large an accumulation of refuse. Unit has been cond. down in very large parties from the TRENCHES. Visited various Sanitary Clinics include DIVISIONAL & 147 Brigade HQ & MOBILE VET SECTION. Also has various billets in FORCEVILLE & HEDAUVILLE cleans up. there being some difficulty in these villages from the rapid movement of troops.	L/Cpl

Army Form C. 2118

WAR DIARY
or
INTELLIGENCE SUMMARY
(Erase heading not required.)

Instructions regarding War Diaries and Intelligence Summaries are contained in F.S. Regs., Part II. and the Staff Manual respectively. Title Pages will be prepared in manuscript.

Place	Date	Hour	Summary of Events and Information	Remarks and references to Appendices
FORCEVILLE	SEPT. 25th		Moved to NEUVILLE — PAS-EN-ARTOIS where we billeted in field. In take over fm 33rd Division as regards area.	WA
"	26th		Finished the move.	WA
"	27th 28th		Detailed Major Thomson to F. tourer villages, visited HENU with the Secretary.	
"	29th		Flew to 33rd Division HQrs. Secretary ment off to examine villages to take over fm to 33 Division all Secretary Inspectors	WA
			viz: FONQUEVILLERS, BIENVILLERS, POMMIER, HUMBERCAMPS, GAUDIEMPRE, SOUSASTRE, ST. AMAND, HEBUTERNE, BAYENCOURT, SAILLY-AU-BOIS, WARLENCOURT, MONDICOURT.	
"	30th		Visited FONQUEVILLERS to inspect the WATER TANKS there mostly in repair.	WA

140/128

49th Divl Sanitary Section

Oct 1916

COMMITTEE FOR THE
MEDICAL HISTORY OF THE WAR
Date -2 DEC. 1916

...dical

War Diary.

49. Divisional
　　Sanitary Section.

Month of October 1916.

MEDICAL
Army Form C. 2118

WAR DIARY
or
INTELLIGENCE SUMMARY

49th (W.R.) Divisional Sanitary Section

Vol 17

(Erase heading not required.)

Place	Date	Hour	Summary of Events and Information	Remarks and references to Appendices
COUTERELLE	Oct 1st 1916		Made arrangements for taking over area between [?] 4th & 1st Division & 40th Div. St AMAND, HEBUTERNE, BAYENCOURT, MONDICOURT & WARLINCOURT from which [?]	
"	2nd			
"	3rd		Visited WARLUZEL, SOMBRIN, COUTERELLE — billets, but it...	
"	4th		arranged to get men for latrines for which 7 Divisional men...	
"	5th		went over area to find out space required at various villages for latrines -	
"	6th		all above arrangements to be cancelled as we moved to the Flanders	
"	7th		look coming.	
"	8th			
"	9th		went round part of area with DADMS (Sanitation) of 3rd ARMY	
"	10th		got a list of all incinerators in the area to hand to ADMS. —	
"	11th			
"	12th		Drew Bricks for making incinerators at WARLUZEL & COULLEMONT &	
"	13th		delivered them at the villages. also got men from RE for	
"	14th		taking latrines at WARLUZEL.	
"	15th		Tested of water supplies in area & troop billeted with.	

WAR DIARY
or
INTELLIGENCE SUMMARY
(Erase heading not required.)

Army Form C. 2118

Instructions regarding War Diaries and Intelligence Summaries are contained in F. S. Regs., Part II. and the Staff Manual respectively. Title Pages will be prepared in manuscript.

Place	Date	Hour	Summary of Events and Information	Remarks and references to Appendices
COUTERELLE	Oct. 16		Visit from men in area COUTERELLE, WARLUZEL, COULEMONT, SOMBRIN — Wells billets &c. — through no road.	MP2
"	17			
"	18			
"	19			
"	20		Finished reconnaissance of COUTERELLE — Brick works from freeco.	MP2
"	21		Began moving to Humbercamp — HENU	
HENU	22		Reconnoitred billet accommodation of SOMBRIN, WARLUZEL, COULEMONT, COUTERELLE and respective to their villages — HEBUTERNE, SOUASTRE, ST. AMAND, SAILLY, BAVENCOURT &c. Took over from 48th Division.	WP
"	23		Relieved billet Reconnoitre of GAUDIEMPRE. But medical particulars to hand now. HENU with A.D.M.S.	MP
"	24		GAUDIEMPRE + SOUASTRE.	
"	25		Sifted our cases upwards from HUMBERCAMP, FONQVILLERS, SOUASTRE, HEBUTERNE. Villages emptied as orsi — FONQVILLERS, SOUASTRE	MP
"	26		HUMBERCAMP. Shrapnel at all billets. Catral this will & turks surveyed, villages being examined.	MP
"	27			
"	28			
"	29			
"	30			

Army Form C. 2118

WAR DIARY
or
INTELLIGENCE SUMMARY
(Erase heading not required.)

Instructions regarding War Diaries and Intelligence Summaries are contained in F. S. Regs., Part II. and the Staff Manual respectively. Title Pages will be prepared in manuscript.

Place	Date	Hour	Summary of Events and Information	Remarks and references to Appendices
HENU.	Oct. 31st 1916	—	Since the 18th Oct., cases have been notified as follows:— There were notified from various villages. Chiefly { FONQVILLERS. HUMBERCAMP. SOUASTRE. HEBUTERNE Also — SOUASTRE + FONQVILLERS have had in most cases. On enquiry from the movements of the affected men from the previous 2 weeks, it appears that SOUASTRE or FONQVILLERS have been the places in common with the majority of HUMBERCAMP men. All billets occupied by the cases have been disinfected — during billets occupied for the previous 2 weeks, + they into "cellars" is the line. Contacts have been isolated + steps taken to keep them to be examined (factory walls). Water supplies have been examined + steps taken to remedy any defects at wells or stop the use of wells likely to be contaminated.	[signature]

Place	Date	Hour	Summary of Events and Information	Remarks and references to Appendices
HENU	31st Oct 1916		In addition measures are being taken to examine the civilians in the affected village. Extensive eating houses, farms where cows are kept, milk is sold — have has all their civilian inhabitants examined & see if there are any suspicious symptoms; enquiries are made as to any history of illness. The village of Smasté has been thus examined and only in those cases then anything suspicious found. In this case; the Town major has been notified that the place is "Out of Bounds" for troops. All the civilians have been warned not to mix with anybody. As soon as Graham arrives their throats will be examined bacteriologically, & the people kept in the town till the results are known. The other villages affected will be treated similarly.	☒

140/1846

49th Divl Sanitary Section

COMMITTEE FOR THE
MEDICAL HISTORY OF THE WAR
Date -3 JAN. 1917

MEDICAL.
Army Form C. 2118

WAR DIARY
or
INTELLIGENCE SUMMARY 49th (W.R.) Divisional Sanitary Section
(Erase heading not required.)

Vol 18

Instructions regarding War Diaries and Intelligence Summaries are contained in F.S. Regs., Part II. and the Staff Manual respectively. Title Pages will be prepared in manuscript.

Place	Date	Hour	Summary of Events and Information	Remarks and references to Appendices
HENU.	Nov. 1st		Finished inspecting civilians in Saulchoy & transit to HUMBERCAMP.	W/f
"	2nd		Went round civilians in HUMBERCAMP & found one suspicious case only — with a history suggestive of DIPHTHERIA	B/f
"	3rd/4th		Visited SOUASTRE & C.C.S. no 43. about 1am wrote for throat swabs.	W/s
"	5th		Visited SOUASTRE & HUMBERCAMP. Took swabs from throats & suspicious cases this	/a
"	6th		Visited HUMBERCAMP & BIENVILLERS. Had a look at some of civilians in the other place.	W/s.
"	7th 8th		Found one of these cases in SOUASTRE among the civilians was "carrier" of it DIPHTHERIA BACILLUS. Informed TOWN MAJOR & had house put out of bounds — also houses next to them, arranged to have this case removed to Civilian Hospital at ST POL for men.	W/t
"	9th		"Carrier" case at SOUASTRE removed to ST POL. Arranged about disinfection of its house.	W/f
"	10		Visited HUMBERCAMP to close down for reasons in aid water.	W/f
"	11		Visited HEBUTERNE & BIENVILLERS. At Letty Place complaints had been made that the incinerator dress fire from Sweeny	W/A

1875 Wt. W593/826 1,000,000 4/15 J.B.C. & A. A.D.S.S./Forms/C. 2118.

WAR DIARY
or
INTELLIGENCE SUMMARY
(Erase heading not required.)

Army Form C. 2118

Place	Date	Hour	Summary of Events and Information	Remarks and references to Appendices
HENU	Nov. 12		Visited SOUASTRE and ST. AMAND	
"	13		Making arrangements to get incinerator built for disposal of rubbish at BIENVILLERS.	
"	14		Building of incinerator in progress, also being pushed on rapidly. Also making of latrine	
"	15		SOAP TRAP for BATHS at HENU hill plans in position. Water supply for area being	
"	16		examined.	
"	17		An incinerator has been built at ST AMAND and another put inside the village has been	
"	18		altered & put into working order. There 2 are to have rubbish for ST AMAND.	
"	19		DIVISION & TOWN MAJOR BIENVILLERS informed. 10 large pick incinerators have been	
"	20		erected in our area up to the present.	
"			Thus I REQUETERNE, SAILLY-au-Bois, BEYENCOURT, HUMBERCAMP, have been going up	
			by the DIVISION and Village of POMMIER taken over.	
			DA to MS (Sanitation) of 3rd ARMY visited our area	
"	21		Visited ST. POL & saw SANITARY EXHIBITS there.	
"	22		Visited ST. AMAND - SOUASTRE. Other work as usual.	
"	23		Visited GAUDIEMPRE, ST. AMAND with ADMS.	
"	24		Visited CCS (43) to see about drain supply for Diphtheria cases also visited	
			WARLINCOURT.	

WAR DIARY
or
INTELLIGENCE SUMMARY

(Erase heading not required.)

Army Form C. 2118

Place	Date	Hour	Summary of Events and Information	Remarks and references to Appendices
HENU	Nov. 25		Visited St. Amand. Otherwise as usual.	
	26		Visited Reserve Trenches of 143rd & 146th Brigades. Also visited MANNESCAMPS and arranged to have a large heap of upper premises to work area to be used. To be done by entire long the same evening.	
	27		Visited GRENAS & visited some billets there. Otherwise as usual	
	28		Visited POMMIER & BIENVILLERS. Had 2 men actg. as Sanitary Inspectors at Bellow place sent to hospital from effects of shell gas. Lietn: delivered at BOUXOTRE. Work as usual.	
	29			
	30		Off on leave (10 days) to England.	

SECRET.

WAR DIARY.

OF

49th (W.R.) Divisional Sanitary Section

FOR

December 1916.

SECRET.

WAR DIARY.

OF

FOR

1917.

Confidential
Medical

War Diary.

49th Line Sanitary Section.

Month of December. 1916.

MEDICAL Army Form C. 2118

49th (W.R.) Divisional Sanitary Section

WAR DIARY
or
INTELLIGENCE SUMMARY
(Erase heading not required.)

Instructions regarding War Diaries and Intelligence Summaries are contained in F.S. Regs., Part II. and the Staff Manual respectively. Title Pages will be prepared in manuscript.

Place	Date	Hour	Summary of Events and Information	Remarks and references to Appendices
HENU	Dec 1st		Work as usual. 2 incinerators at SOUASTRE in Valley Camp finished and latrines constructed also. New Hut erected by SANITARY SECTION H.Q. at HENU.	WB
	to Dec 11th			WB
	12th		Moved to LUCHEUX. (Sheet 51.C. T.16.)	
LUCHEUX	13th		O.C. On Leave. arrived back late at night.	
	14th 15th		Work carried on as usual. Scheme to make all latrines fly proof in area. HALLOY - GRENAS - BEAUREPAIRE - MONDICOURT - POMMERA - GROUCHES - MILLY - LUCHEUX started.	
	16		Visited HALLOY incinerators fly stove. Also visited ST-POL - Sanitary Conference.	
	17		Visited GRENAS re sanitary arrangements for DIVISIONAL SCHOOL erected there	
	18		Visited HALLOY again re incinerators.	BA
	19		Visited GROUCHES and + BOUT DE PRES re incinerators.	WD
	20		Visited POMMERA — incinerators.	

1375 Wt. W593/826 1,000,000 4/15 J.B.C. & A. A.D.S.S./Forms/C. 2118.

Army Form C. 2118

WAR DIARY
or
INTELLIGENCE SUMMARY
(Erase heading not required.)

Instructions regarding War Diaries and Intelligence Summaries are contained in F.S. Regs., Part II. and the Staff Manual respectively. Title Pages will be prepared in manuscript.

Place	Date	Hour	Summary of Events and Information	Remarks and references to Appendices
LUCHEUX.	Dec. 21st		Visited BEAUREPAIRE FARM + HALLOY — a reconnaissance	
"	22		" GRENAS — Reconnaissance.	
"	23rd		" MONDICOURT, HALLOY, Primus Camps and MILLY — a reconnaissance. (Christmas Day of United HALLOY - improved in afternoon).	
"	28		Visited LE GROS TILON FARM + Camp + LUCHEUX — a reconnaissance	
"	29		Visited HUMBERCOURT — a reconnaissance & was seen. Stated yellow de Calais front is bad area	
"	30		Visited HUMBERCOURT and WARLUZEL — a reconnaissance	
"	31		Visited POMMERA, MONDICOURT, GRENAS, HALLOY to see proper funds to putting up Latrines.	

W.W. Adamson Capt. R.Army.C
O.C. San. Section 49 Divn.

1375 Wt. W593/826 1,000,000 4/15 J.B.C. & A. A.D.S.S./Forms/C. 2118.

140/9+1 Vol 20.

Jan 1917 SECRET.

WAR DIARY.

OF

H.q.th Divisional Sanitary Section

FOR

1917.

January

COMMITTEE FOR THE
MEDICAL HISTORY OF THE WAR
Date 13 MAR. 1917

WAR DIARY.

OF

FOR

1917.

SECRET.

War Diary

49th Divisional Sanitary Section

For Month of January 1917.

SECRET
Medical

MEDICAL.

Army Form C. 2118

WAR DIARY
or
INTELLIGENCE SUMMARY

49th (W.R.) Division Sanitary Section

(Erase heading not required.)

Instructions regarding War Diaries and Intelligence Summaries are contained in F. S. Regs., Part II. and the Staff Manual respectively. Title Pages will be prepared in manuscript.

Place	Date	Hour	Summary of Events and Information	Remarks and references to Appendices
LUCHEUX	Jan'y 1st 2nd 3rd		Visited various camps near LUCHEUX, also HALLOY, LE GRES TION PAIE and MONDICOURT. Hut firing & latrines in use were being proceeded with.	
	4th 5th 6th		Visited SUS. ST.LEGER in reconnaissance Visited GROUCHES, MILLY, went round LUCHEUX, also MONDICOURT. The area has been practically cleaned — only defect remaining, lack of latrines for 4 sects each to be made of this village, shields no pit for the dry pit.	
	7th		LE GRES THON FARM CAMP. Dwelling is this area now from goo Latrines that have been made by the Sanitary Section is found in position now fit. which have been aug mented at the top. Bulk of plans have been made of the area HALLOY – PREUNE – BEAUREPAIRE – AUMERA – MONDICOURT GROUCHES – MILLY, BOUT DE PRES – LUCHEUX – LE GRES THON FARM. The shewed sites of latrines (which were built & placed in position before leaving the area) Alterations made — all of what were shown by the OC. of the Sanitary Section in connection with the Engineers working these villages, examining these camps. The SANITARY SECTION handed over to the 30th Division SANITARY SECTION & obtained receipts for all stores & work its left in the workshops.	
	8th		Finished move of Sect. to BAVINCOURT Sheet 51c. P. 34. b. + d.	

Army Form C. 2118

WAR DIARY
or
INTELLIGENCE SUMMARY
(Erase heading not required.)

Instructions regarding War Diaries and Intelligence Summaries are contained in F. S. Regs., Part II. and the Staff Manual respectively. Title Pages will be prepared in manuscript.

Place	Date	Hour	Summary of Events and Information	Remarks and references to Appendices
BAYINCOURT	Jan 9th		Sanitary Inspectors were sent out to SAULTY. LA CAUCHIE. BAILLEULVAL. LATBRET. BERLES. GROSVILLE. HUMBERCAMPS. COULLEMONT. BAILLEULMONT. BASSEUX.	App.
"	10th		mainly occupied in cleaning up latrines and collecting information regarding BATHS.	App.
"	11th		LATRINGS, INCINERATORS, etc.	App.
"	"		visited BAILLEULMONT and BAILLEUVAL.	App.
"	13th		visited LA CAUCHIE — went into villages	App.
"	14th		visited GROSVILLE — have visited village.	App.
"	15th		BAILLEULMONT again — went into villages choosing sites for latrines. also	App.
"	16th		visited HUMBERCAMP — went into village. DROMS (Sanitary) ARMY came and visited — viz: — BAYINCOURT, LA CAUCHIE, BAILLEULMONT, BAILLEUVAL	App.
"	17th		LA CAUCHIE & HUMBERCAMP again.	
"	18th		In this new area comparatively little with the trenches appears to have been done. All manure has been left heaped up at the trenches — seemingly for months, and the latrines are all in the bucket system with small wooden cans or no cans at all. It is not a satisfactory method of keeping the latrines fly-proof. The whole area will have to be reorganised & latrines made for the whole area.	App.

Army Form C. 2118

WAR DIARY
or
INTELLIGENCE SUMMARY
(Erase heading not required.)

Instructions regarding War Diaries and Intelligence Summaries are contained in F. S. Regs., Part II. and the Staff Manual respectively. Title Pages will be prepared in manuscript.

Place	Date	Hour	Summary of Events and Information	Remarks and references to Appendices
BAVINCOURT	Jan 20		Visited JPBL + gave lectures on FLIES, LICE, DISINFECTION etc etc.	#1
"	21"		ditto ditto BAVINCOURT —	#1
"	22"		Visited ST POL for SANITARY CONFERENCE there.	
"	23"		Visited HUMBERCAMP, LA CAUVERIE, BAILLEUL MONT — where much cleaner. Burning + coal	#2
"	24"		camps & much as usual.	
"	25"		Another team in from camps as very much beyond cleaning up LATRINES are	#2
"	26"		for mules. Visited CAMPS near LA BAZEQUE showing the latrines	
"	27		Visited LA BAZEQUE FAYE & CHATEAU —	
"	28"		Visited hordes no chance left it the — but very bad.	#3
"	29		LA BAZEQUE FARM & CHATEAU — An attempt to get anthrax toxint + culture collected	#3
"	30"		LA BAZEQUE FARM seen a case of suspected Dysentery there.	#2
"	31"		Divisional manure dumps have been established — one to each 2 villages.	#3
			These have been staffed by 7 men to each — the manure stacked up into a large space	
			men + teats aided. All small dumps to marked to all manure is deposited there by units	

W.H. Adamson Captain
O.C. Sanitary Section
49

SECRET.

WAR DIARY.

OF

Hq^{rs} (W.R.) Div^{l} Sanitary Section.

FOR

February 1917.

SECRET.

28.2.17.

The A.D.M.S.
49th Div.

WAR DIARY.

Month ending February 28th 1917.

W W Adamson

Capt. R.A.M.C. (T)
O.C. 49th Div. Sanitary Sectn.

WAR DIARY or INTELLIGENCE SUMMARY

Army Form C. 2118

MEDICAL

49¹ (W.R) Div. Sanitary Section

Place	Date	Hour	Summary of Events and Information	Remarks and references to Appendices
BAVINCOURT	Feb 1		Visited BAILLEULMONT, BAILLEUVAL, LA CAUCHIE,	
	2		took in village of RIVIERE + LE FERMONT + WAILLY and sub-visited inspection here.	
	3		The weather has stopped work in certain directions as the hard frost makes it	
	4		very difficult to dig in the ground. Also the trenches covered up with the snow	
			upon which cannot be found to funnels to men to be left till the thaw	
			comes. Visited St POL re pre lecture of S.A.O. Sanity Sanitation.	
	Feb 6		Visited GROSVILLE, BRETENCOURT, BAILLEULMONT, BASSEUX, BAILLEUVAL.	
	7		Visited Camp at B.22.c. Shut 51.C. — arrangements for latrines here in	
	8		camp not by... The Bodea has destroyed the tents to the LAUNDRY to disinfect	
	9		clothes — the circular tents being frozen. Occupied by 148th Brigade — also those in its	
	10		visited trenches in middle sector. Occupied by the 147th Brigade. Kitchens fairly clean.	
			left.	
	Feb 11		Visited HUMBERCAMP, LA CAUCHIE, GROSVILLE, BELLACOURT, BAILLEUVAL, BASSEUX.	
	12		Latrines are being gradually changed to the fly-proof box-cum-urinal pits. So far	
	13		sufficient for about 4,000 men have been erected — in eight Section Zones. Here the	
	14		also visited 146th Brigade line.	
	15		trenches Iron middens stand in the left.	
			so as result from seeing the trenches — Interim report on recommend-	
			ation they fly-proof boxes shall be made, one for 5 feet deep in the top section	
			when the ground was dry to top-soil firm and rather porous	
			in the right + centre sector where the soil was clay wet the bucket type	
			or the French latrine was advised.	

WAR DIARY
or
INTELLIGENCE SUMMARY.
(Erase heading not required.)

Army Form C. 2118.

49²(WR) Div. Sanitary Section

Place	Date	Hour	Summary of Events and Information	Remarks and references to Appendices
BAVINCOURT	Feb. 17		Hotel ST. POL. Kpri Lecture at 3rd Army School of Sanitation.	#
"	"18		The Army has commenced, and the school will in course of time arrive is	#
"	"19		Inspection of K. flour study	#
"	"20		The villages BAVINCOURT, HUMBERCAMP, BAILLEULVAL, & LE FERMONT. Visited HUMBERCAMP, BAILLEULVAL, & LE FERMONT.	#
"	"21		Visited H.Q. of 58" Division & OC San Sect of that Division returned his visit afterwards & he handed over in connection for a new hut & the workshop	#
"	"22		Inspecting return in all material to be handed over, all took a hard while down ets.	#
"	"23		Visited LA CAUCHIE. Visited LA CAUCHIE + near.	#
"	"24		Handing over various villages to 58" Division Sanitary Section. Having some slight of having found them disinfected	#
"	"25		Packing up. Finishing all return etc.	#
"	"26		Moved to LUCHEUX with Div. Headquarters.	#
LUCHEUX	"27		Remained at LUCHEUX - wet of day.	#
"	"28		Moved to BONNIERES (S.W. of FREVENT) with half section + half of them. LORRY on top of Lift at LUCHEUX (The returns). LORRY on if new set off of HUMBERCOURT to BOUQEMAISON. — Stuck on it FODEN LORRY sent off from HUMBERCOURT to BOUQEMAISON. — Stuck on it road at MILLY (E. of DOULLENS).	#

W. Foreman Capt RAMC
O.C. San Sect

Vol 22

140/1043.

COMMITTEE FOR THE
MEDICAL HISTORY OF THE WAR
Date 11 MAY.1917

S E C R E T.

W A R D I A R Y.

OF

Sanitary Section 49th (WR) Division

F O R

March 1917.

MEDICAL.

Army Form C. 2118.

WAR DIARY
or
INTELLIGENCE SUMMARY. 49th (West Riding) Div. Sanitary Section

(Erase heading not required.)

Instructions regarding War Diaries and Intelligence Summaries are contained in F. S. Regs., Part II. and the Staff Manual respectively. Title pages will be prepared in manuscript.

Place	Date	Hour	Summary of Events and Information	Remarks and references to Appendices
LUCHEUX	March 1st		Marched to HERNICOURT	
HERNICOURT	2nd		" " PERNES	
PERNES	3rd		Section marched to HAVERSKERQUE. O.C. San. Section proceeded to LA GORGUE to arrange taking over from 56th Division San. Section O.C.	
LA GORGUE	4th		Section moved to LA GORGUE. Main Group arrived over with O.C. Sn. Section. 56th Div.	
	5th		(LA GORGUE = L.35. A.1.3. Sheet 36.A.) Visited LAVENTIE.	
	6th		56th Div. San. Section moved away.	
	7th		Went round LA GORGUE - saw part of sector S.P.H. which consist mostly of	
	8th		Visited lines of Centre Brigade. (Tanks & [shallow?] pumps & wells.	
	9th		Forden Lorry arrived at LA GORGUE.	
	10th		Visited Div. School at MERVILLE. The 9-man Lorry of LA GORGUE ? LAVENTIE have now got their Sanitary arrangements organised	
	11th		Visited BEAUPRÉ - proposer of new Camp - reference a case of Dysentery. Left for England on Special Leave sent report in to Adms.	
	23rd		Returned from England.	

WAR DIARY
or
INTELLIGENCE SUMMARY.
(Erase heading not required.)

Army Form C. 2118.

Place	Date	Hour	Summary of Events and Information	Remarks and references to Appendices
LA GORGUE	24		Visited LA GORGUE village.	
"	25		Visited LESTREM — went round some responsibilities Chris large accumulation of manure and dirt.	
"	26		Visited Left Brigade hrs - right sector with reference to their water supply.	
"	27		Conference at A.D.M.S. Office. Collected all reports on water supplies on front line together for our report.	
"	28		Visited MERVILLE — Div. School — gave lecture on Sanitation there.	
"	29		Visited RIEZ BAILLEUL, PONT DU HEM and LE DRUMEZ — seeing various. Where there were large accumulations of manure and visited billets. Also have head safes in town & have the Cahier fly-proof. Arrange to have head safes in town & have the Cahier fly-proof.	
"	30		Visited Centre Brigade right sector to see some surveys of ruffs. L. Rich Serre rd. antipyretics.	
"	31		Visited VIEILLE CHAPELLE — examine into cases of nephritis in village — Examine civilians — also visited civilians who were ill.	Capt.

W.T. Hammond
G.P. 49th Div. San. Sect.

www.ingramcontent.com/pod-product-compliance
Lightning Source LLC
Chambersburg PA
CBHW081423160426
43193CB00013B/2178